A Donkey On The Catwalk

Tales of life in Greece

(Fourth book in the Peloponnese series)

By Marjory McGinn

Pelagos Press

A Donkey On The Catwalk

Published by Pelagos Press, 2021.

ISBN: 978-1-9999957-5-1

Cover illustration by Tony Hannaford (www.anthonyhannaford.co.uk).

Editing, formatting and author photographs by Jim Bruce (www.ebooklover.co.uk).

About the author

Marjory McGinn is a Scottish-born author and journalist, brought up in Australia. She worked in Sydney as senior feature writer on *The Sun-Herald* and as a freelance writer in Scotland for 10 years from 2000. Her work has appeared in leading newspapers in Britain and Australia, including *The Daily Mail*, *The Times*, *The Daily Telegraph*, *The Herald* and *The Sydney Morning Herald*.

A youthful work/travel year in Athens inspired a lifelong fascination for Greece. In 2010, together with her husband Jim and their terrier Wallace, she set off for an adventure in the southern Peloponnese that lasted four years and was the basis for her travel memoirs starting with the Amazon best-seller *Things Can Only Get Feta*. Her second travel memoir, *Homer's Where The Heart Is*, also a best-seller, was voted one of the best expat books for 2015 by the Displaced Nation website. Stories about her travels in Greece have also appeared in the *Evening Times*, *The Scotsman*, *Neos Kosmos* newspaper in Australia, *Womankind* magazine, and the Athens-based *Dimokratia* newspaper.

Marjory is a Member of The Society of Authors in London and also writes a blog with a Greek and travel theme on the website www.bigfatgreekodyssey.com and she can be followed on Twitter www.twitter.com/@fatgreekodyssey and Facebook www.facebook.com/MarjoryMcGinnAuthor.

Other books by Marjory McGinn

The Peloponnese series
Things Can Only Get Feta
Homer's Where The Heart Is
A Scorpion In The Lemon Tree

The Bronte In Greece series
A Saint For The Summer
How Greek Is Your Love?

Dedication

To my late father, John McGinn

Note – Modern Greek

Modern Greek is a complex language and some word forms may confuse readers. Basically, articles, nouns, adjectives and pronouns change with gender, number and position in sentence.

The noun *xenos*, for example, meaning foreigner in the masculine form sometimes appears in the text in plural, as *xenoi*.

Masculine names that end in 'os' or 'is' will drop the final 's' in the vocative case when addressing someone. The name Vassilis for example will change to: 'Vassili, are you listening?'

Greek words used in this book are generally written as they would be pronounced in Greek.

"When you set out on the voyage to Ithaka
Pray that the way be long
Full of adventures and experiences
The Laistrygonians, and the Kyklopes,
Angry Poseidon – don't be afraid of them"

– from Ithaka, by Greek poet Konstantinos Kavafis

Contents

Map of the region

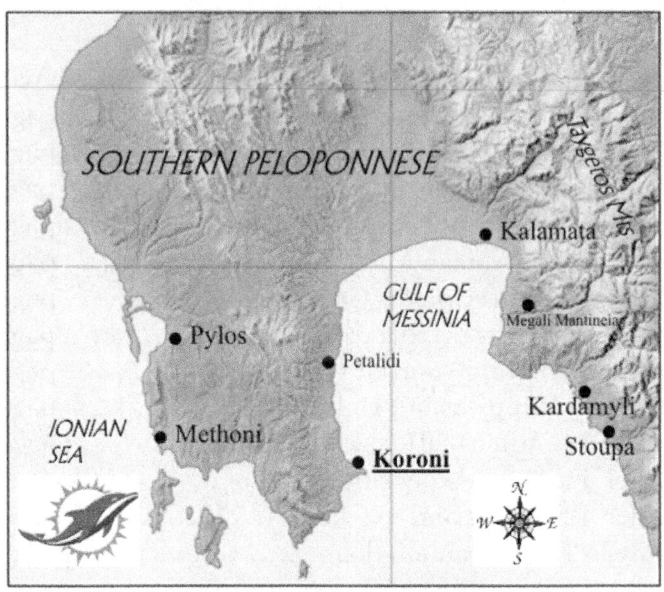

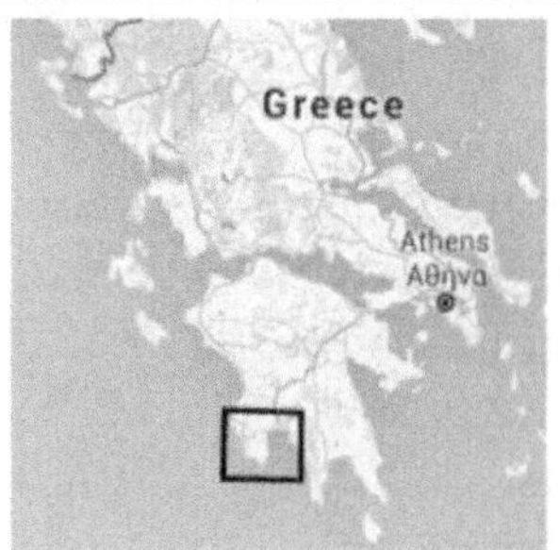

Preface

IN the spring of 2010 my husband Jim and I, along with our Jack Russell terrier, Wallace, embarked on the biggest odyssey of our lives. Undeterred by the start of the economic crisis that was engulfing Greece, we moved from a Scottish village to the wild Mani region, in the southern mainland of Greece. We rented a house for a year in a hillside village and then moved to a few other locations in this region, all of which lasted four years and which I have written about in my Peloponnese series, starting with the Amazon best-seller *Things Can Only Get Feta*.

A Donkey On The Catwalk (the fourth in the series) is a book of original stories, travel narratives and reflections, both comical and thought-provoking, that dip once more into our time in southern Greece and highlight the fascinating and often crazy business of living in that country. The book also contains narratives of other trips to islands such as Santorini and Corfu, and the mainland, and delves into some of my own earlier trips to Greece in past decades, including a youthful and exciting work year in Athens during a dangerous time of political upheaval, and a long sabbatical in Crete that didn't quite go to plan.

At least one of the characters from my memoirs, Foteini the inimitable goat farmer, appears again in this collection, for a compelling reason. Foteini has attracted more attention and fan mail than any other Greek villager I've written about. Many readers have commented on Foteini and asked for updates on her life, and so I have written a chapter about her to start this collection. I have pulled together some disparate threads from my books and written some new and funny anecdotes for those who love hearing about her. I hope I've managed to get a little further under the skin of this unique woman and some of her hilarious habits, such as washing peeled bananas, designing strange footwear, and indulging her beloved donkey Riko with 'fashionable' coats and other strange accessories – hence the title of the book. It was Foteini, who for me became a metaphor for all that is quirky, endearing and often unknowable about Greece.

Some of the stories in this book started out as blog pieces I wrote for our popular website Big Fat Greek Odyssey but have been reworked and expanded for this edition. One of these pieces was included because it brought such an unexpected response from readers. It's a bizarre tale about the church of Ayia Theodora in Arcadia and the 'miracle' of a mini forest sprouting from its roof with a strange Byzantine back story. It's one of the many quirky phenomena I've come across during a lifetime of wandering through Greece.

One of the last stories in this collection is a personal piece about the remarkable fact that in writing my first novel, *A Saint For The Summer,* set in Greece with a World War Two narrative thread, it led to the discovery of my own father's war experiences in the RAF Regiment. It has a surprising Greek connection too. I have included the piece also as a tribute to my father John McGinn, of whom I'm immensely proud. He spoke little about his difficult war years but was one of the many millions of ordinary British servicemen and women who made heroic contributions to the war effort.

I hope you will find something both amusing and informative in this book to pique your interest in this great country, and it may inspire you to embark on a Greek odyssey of your own once some semblance of normality returns after the harrowing events of 2020/21. I hope you enjoy the book, and if you do, please let me know. I love to hear from readers.

Marjory McGinn, Cornwall, England, 2021

1

There's something about Foteini

ONE morning, a few months after moving to a hillside village in the Mani, we saw our friend Foteini on the road, wearing what looked like a bizarre Cornish pasty on one foot. We were taking our dog Wallace for a stroll past Foteini's *ktima*, farm compound. Jim and I looked at each other and laughed when we saw her.

"What the hell is Foteini wearing?" Jim asked.

"No idea. But whatever it is, there'll be a crazy explanation, that's for sure."

We'd become used to the strange way this pensioner lived her life on her goat farm, a ramshackle place full of rural junk and a clutter of plastic chairs and a rickety table, where she served coffee to friends. It was the way she dressed that mainly set Foteini apart from other village women. It was clear she cared not a jot what people thought of her, or her behaviour.

In the first few weeks of our stay in Megali Mantineia, one of the villagers had described Foteini as eccentric, which was ironic in an environment that fizzed so often with eccentricity. It's a Greek word, *ekkentrikotita.* It literally means to be 'outside the centre'. The origin of the word makes perfect sense to me because Greece has mastered the art of eccentricity in many forms: histrionic Olympian gods and goddesses; Orthodox monks who often led bizarre lives, such as the 9th century hermit monk Symeon of Lesvos, known as a *stilitis* because he lived permanently at the top of a stone column in a life of grim abstinence. And there are many modern eccentric characters too, such as off-beat hero Zorba the Greek, inspired by a real character, a man of outlandish enterprises who eschewed rule books of every kind. But Foteini was something else. She had flung herself so far outside the centre she was a satellite settlement of her own.

It was her dress sense that mostly flagged up her eccentric tendencies: her clashing layers – brash florals and paisleys mixed with tartans – and her crazy needlework. She would patch a hole in the bum of black work trousers in big baby stitches of bright red or yellow coloured thread.

But this new shoe creation was something we'd never seen before. She hobbled towards us on the pasty, an old welly boot on the other foot. The pasty appeared to be a flat shoe bound up in a piece of thick, discoloured plastic, the two ends pulled up on top of the foot and stitched together with some kind of twine. It left an inch or so of scalloped plastic rising up like the wavy pastry edge of the savoury Cornish fare we all love. In this instance, the results were outlandish, even for her.

"Have you been walking about like that all morning?" I asked her.

"Yes," she said, giving me a squinty look as if it were a ridiculous question. I shook my head. As the Cornish would say, she'd 'gone Bodmin', bonkers. I had a vision in my head of her plodding up the road, and possibly into the village, looking like some comically dressed Shakespearean eccentric, Malvolio perhaps in *Twelfth Night* with his garish cross-gartered stockings.

"Why are you wearing that ... *thing*?" I asked her. No need to even explain what a pasty was, or the place from where it originated. Geography wasn't her strong point, but we got a brief story about a welly gone to hell that morning and the pasty shoe scrambled together because she needed stout footwear to go to nearby overgrown fields to collect spring greens, *horta,* for her dinner.

"This will do," she said, with an admiring glance as she dug the toe of the pasty idly into the dusty edge of the road.

But Foteini didn't confine her fashion creations just to herself in this Maniot atelier, she also fashioned bizarre but practical outfits for her beloved donkey Riko. She made raincoats for him in winter out of old sheets of plastic with dubious provenance, so she could continue to ride him up and down the village road in all weathers while he was stacked high with firewood. One summer she fashioned a covering to put over his back, under the stout wooden saddle, to keep out the worse of the heat and flies. It seemed to be an oversized buttoned-up spotted dress, the sleeves still hanging limply on either side of the beast's back, the outfit fastened under his belly. Obviously, it was something she'd been gifted by one of the senior villagers with a taste for these perfunctory frocks.

My favourite accessory was the straw hat she fashioned from an old sun hat I'd given her. She made holes for the donkey's ears and tied the hat under its chin. Brilliant really!

To see Riko traipsing down the village road in some new bit of hapless couture, as if he were on a fringe edition of a Paris catwalk, was one of the delights of living in rural Mani. It was easy to see how the villagers had dubbed this widower in her early 60s an eccentric. Yet for all that, Foteini is striking to look at. She has high cheekbones, light blue eyes with fashionably luxurious eyebrows, and she resembles a slightly weather-beaten version of the actress Ingrid Bergman. But there the comparison ends.

Living in Megali Mantineia from 2010 during Greece's economic crisis had brought us a wealth of new, and often mad, experiences that as a journalist I could never have imagined. Many of them involved Foteini but other experiences were bound up with the maverick and innovative way these Maniot folk dealt with their harsh working life: harvesting vast olive orchards, farming goats and sheep on the hillsides, and now having to cope with austerity measures during the economic crisis. I was eager to weave these experiences into articles I planned to write for overseas publications to help fund our Greek odyssey.

However, it was the developing and unlikely friendship with Foteini that turned my creative desires towards something more – a book. Even in this wild and remote slice of Maniot life, I knew that Foteini was quite unique, not just in her behaviour, but I sensed she had a rich store of interesting tales and observations, particularly about her early life in the high Taygetos mountain village of Altomira. It was from here that her family, and many others in the village, had come from to find an easier kind of life near the sea.

I was excited from the beginning at the prospect of winkling out her stories, despite my rusty Greek. So boning up from Greek language books suddenly became a necessary part of each day. I was further motivated by the knowledge that there were few people like Foteini left in southern Greece, who worked their land and hundreds of olive trees alone, using a donkey as the main form of transport. I wanted to record something about her life before it disappeared from this part of Greece forever, especially due to the changes the crisis was bringing.

During our first autumn and winter, when storms blew in from the Taygetos mountains, it was easy to hunker down in our small stone house to write articles, and at the same time I jotted down the first chapters of what would become my first travel memoir, *Things Can Only Get Feta*. I knew that Foteini would be a significant part of the narrative, but what I didn't imagine was that she would become an unlikely muse for the book, and the others that followed: the kind of alternative 'goddess' muse the ancient Greek gods would have toyed with for a while and then flung down from Mount Olympus onto a pitiable and barren hillside, much like Foteini's own farm compound – junk-filled and scrappy, where goats danced on tin roofs and donkeys wore bizarre outfits.

I also didn't anticipate that Foteini would become the star of the first book, along with crazy Wallace the terrier. After *Feta* was published, I received emails to our website, many about Foteini, with comments about her various escapades and questions about her life. After we returned to the UK in 2015, I gave a few talks about our Greek adventures to women's reading groups. I remember one talk in a wealthy village in East Sussex, where I expected the assembled matrons to want anecdotes about Greece in crisis, or perhaps politics. But everyone wanted to know more about Foteini. What she was like, what she ate, and what she wore. Wore? "How long have we got?" I said. Yet I wasn't surprised. Who doesn't want to hear about a Mediterranean battler like Foteini living an unimaginably tough but fascinating life, so unlike our own, a woman who can fashion a shoe like a Cornish pasty when she's never seen one, let alone eaten one?

For me, one of the most astonishing things about Foteini was that she and I became friends in the first place, given that my Greek (having first learnt it during a youthful year in Athens) was rusty at the beginning, and while it improved vastly during that four-year period, communication was rarely easy. Her mountain dialect was hard to understand and she had the rural habit of chopping the ends off many words or running words together, which meant I had to ask her to repeat herself many times until I got the gist of things. She never complained, never gave up in exasperation, but was always mildly amused. Nevertheless, I saw so much of her in the first few years, I feel sure I now have, during excitable moments chattering in Greek, a trace of Maniot goat farmer in my speech.

She could be irascible at times. One day when we were visiting her *ktima*, on the edge of the village, I went over to see Riko, who was tethered under an olive tree. I'd brought a bag of carrots with me that had lost a bit of freshness but were fine for the donkey – or so I thought. I started snapping them in half and feeding them to Riko. Foteini raced over.

"What are you doing, Margarita?" This was the name she'd christened me with because like most Greeks she couldn't pronounce the 'j' in Marjory. "Why are you giving Riko *karota*? You'll make him sick." She pulled a face like curdled milk.

"Don't be silly. Donkeys love carrots. They won't do him any harm," I said, with slight exasperation.

"Show me the bag," she said peevishly.

I handed her the plastic bag of carrots. She looked inside, pulled a few out, turned them this way and that, then sniffed them, as if she'd never seen carrots before.

"Don't give them to Riko. I'm having these for my evening meal," she said, marching off with the bag to squirrel away in her shed. I shook my head in amusement. The normally good-natured donkey kicked out at his water trough, which was an old Feta cheese tin repurposed. I felt his pain.

Foteini could be blunt as well, but always comically so. Once at her *ktima* we'd been standing around talking when she suddenly went quiet and stood right in front of me, gawping at my teeth, looking at them from every angle, her face scrunched like a petulant dentist.

"You've got false teeth, haven't you?" she said loudly.

"No I haven't."

"They're nice, but I can tell they're false."

I laughed and didn't know whether to take it as an insult or a compliment, as I don't have false teeth. Foteini had a thing about teeth and hers were, for a poor goat farmer, quite good. She looked after them and once told me how much she was paying for a complicated bit of dental work after she lost a tooth on a hard toffee when an expat neighbour gave her a box of chocolates. I admired the fact that beneath the gruff exterior a little healthy vanity was still in evidence and the dental work would have bitten mightily into her modest savings, if she had any.

Occasionally when Jim was busy at the house, writing up a freelance article or indulging one of his new hobbies, like pickling olives or refining his signature moussaka dish, I would go alone to the *ktima* to see how Foteini was getting on, especially if I was having an unproductive or gloomy day because she always cheered me up with dizzy antics, or some peculiar observation on life. Although she had a crumbling village house nearby, where she slept at night, she could generally be found in daytime hours at her farm compound.

One day I spent a few hours with her there, sheltering from heavy rain in the musty *kaliva,* shack, where she stored animal fodder, and had a collection of ancient crockery and cutlery and other items of indeterminate usage in a heavy chest of drawers. She also had a *petrogazi,* a two-ring cooker, set on a rough table. While making Greek coffee she manhandled the cooker, suspecting a gas blockage from the bottle below and in her impatience nearly blew the shack up.

When I look back, I wonder what on earth we prattled on about for hours. While I call it a friendship, two people were never so different, as if we'd come from different planets, let alone cultures. Yet we did talk, and quite often about her early mountain life, her former husband, her fears about the many challenges of life in the crisis. Her vulnerability on the farm was also a source of pained discussion. During the crisis, when austerity spawned plenty of opportunistic burglars, Foteini's *ktima* was broken into and some of her goats were slaughtered on site and stolen for their meat, which the police did little to investigate. She often feared for the future, but when kindly villagers suggested she should retire, she would harrumph and say things like, "What would I do? Sit at home all day and do *kentima* (embroidery)?" And then she would laugh vibrantly. Having seen her efforts with needlework, I doubted it was an option.

More recently, Foteini was attacked in her village home in a shocking incident. She was tied up and her place was ransacked, as if she had been sitting on a fat nest egg of money. Yet Foteini had nothing of value, or of interest to anyone. It was decided in the village that the intruder had been one of the growing number of itinerants who roam about rural Greece looking for work, or an easy break-in, and no-one has been charged with the crime. As far as I have gleaned, no investigation of the incident has even taken place.

"The local police don't like investigating rural crimes in the Mani. They think it's a waste of resources," one doughty village elder told me.

Foteini's life was sometimes more complex than I could ever imagine, as I wrote in more depth in *Things Can Only Get Feta*. For all her toughness and eccentricities, there was a wisdom about her that cut refreshingly through all the triteness of modern life. I remember her once lamenting the loss of a village friend. I found her sitting on a rock in one of her fields and she told me she'd been to the funeral a few days earlier. She looked understandably glum and contemplative, not a mood I'd often seen her in. She bent over and touched the long skinny stem of a purple wildflower.

"That's all we are, Margarita, a silly flower like this, alive a few days and then ... finished!" she said, ripping the scrawny bloom out of the ground with strange ferocity.

She tossed the flower aside and scraped her foot around on the ground, stirring up dust. Despite the context, I found the moment blackly amusing: Foteini summing up the whole of life and death with one blow from her big meaty hand.

It wasn't every day Foteini had philosophical musings and her dark mood didn't last long, but the incident left me with a new insight into her world and how narrow her expectations of life must have been most of the time: that life wouldn't offer her very much, and then a swift scything at the end. Her raw, pared-down slant on life continued to intrigue me for years and it was so at odds with our own western notions of entitlement, our obsession with personal rights and freedom, and our acquisitiveness.

Her approach was something that I drew on in my travel memoirs and later in my two novels, also set in the Mani. I can't deny she was partly the inspiration for the comical Myrto, also a goat farmer, in the novels. And in many ways some might even say Foteini has been slightly, creatively repurposed into this rural character, although it wouldn't be true. Myrto is her own woman and more street-wise, with an Australian back story, and has more levity about her. But Foteini and Myrto definitely have a similar provenance.

My friendship with Foteini was challenging and a point of reference that stayed with me for the whole of our odyssey and beyond. It taught me one thing above all else: that in order to really change your life, even for a short time, you need to go beyond your comfort zone with places and with people. It was a lesson I had started to learn painfully some years earlier when I took up horse-riding in Scotland as an adult and initially found it terrifying, as well as exhilarating. I finally grasped the fact that if you have a horse you trust, you must have the faith to just go with it. Let it have its head. It was a good metaphor for life. But in Greece with Foteini, and other locals I met, sometimes I had to go *way* beyond what was comfortable, or even normal, especially during the crisis, when even Greeks were taking a flying leap into the unknown.

Foteini was a pragmatic soul at heart. There was no fey, idealised Arcadian wood nymph about her and she was shrewd when she wanted to be, and mischievous. A couple of times we helped her with her winter olive harvest, just for a day here and there. We were novices and it was back-breaking work. This was something she mostly did herself every year on several hundred trees, or occasionally with the help of a few casual labourers. We did it out of friendship and to experience the harvest.

"I'm going to buy you both some souvlaki for this at the Kali Kardia," she told us after we finished helping with the harvest. The Kali Kardia (The Good Heart) was the local *kafeneio*, which is a traditional kind of coffee shop in Greece where men gather to play cards, or families go for refreshments after Sunday church services. Frequently, these places also serve simple Greek meals.

"Next week, we'll go, eh Margarita?"

We told her she didn't have to do that, to repay our bumbling efforts at olive-picking. The week came and went and every week after that she would refresh the promise. "Next week, Margarita, we'll go for that souvlaki..." And still nothing happened. This went on and on for months and each time it was mentioned we'd say, "*O, ti theleis*. Whatever you want!"

In the end it became an amusing ritual between us – a funny rural chant until it was dropped, for reasons I can't quite remember, or perhaps the enthusiasm for the invitation had simply timed out in her mind and was forgotten, not because she was ungrateful or mean. On many visits to her *ktima*, she gave us olive oil and cheese, and probably would have given us the badly darned tartan shirt off her back if we'd asked for it. I began to think that deep down Foteini was just shy and unused to socialising widely, as if she felt herself to be in an alien world.

Our friendship with her was not only curious to us but it intrigued the rest of the village at times, the Greeks mostly. In their eyes Foteini had the status of a *paradosiaki yinaika*, a traditional woman, and definitely not someone they imagined a foreigner would spark with: living alone, no children, doing her own thing, keeping animals, talking to goats. There are other women in rural Greece outwardly similar to Foteini in some ways: widows eking out a living alone, and sometimes a trifle eccentric. But there was also an otherness to Foteini I never absolutely grasped because of my imperfect Greek. And perhaps that was the thread that united Foteini and us, and Wallace too, because we were all 'other', aliens, *xenoi*, for different reasons.

Although we met many other wonderful villagers and went to church services with them, were invited into their homes and stayed in touch with them for years, we still felt, even after four years, that sense of otherness which most foreigners feel to a certain extent – living in a distant land, particularly in less sophisticated rural areas like the Mani. This is an area that is historically tough, riven by clan wars, suspicious of outsiders, and wild, even to other mainland Greeks.

Sadly, not everyone was polite about our curious friendship with Foteini. One village elder on the way back from a church service collared me and asked rather brusquely why we bothered with an uneducated woman like Foteini, given our profession and background, when there were more interesting, clever people in the village. I felt shocked and slightly hectored by the question, though not surprised.

"We know many other people in the village too," I said, setting him straight. "But we think Foteini's terrific. We've never met anyone like her anywhere." He looked stunned, insulted I thought, or maybe ashamed. I couldn't tell. But I changed the subject because I didn't have the skill to try to analyse the friendship in Greek for this man, and to be honest, I didn't completely understand it myself. Nor did I need to.

To the end though, Foteini continued to surprise me, and sometimes confuse me, notwithstanding the inadequacies of my language skills. After *Things Can Only Get Feta* was published, featuring a wonderful illustration of her riding Riko on the book cover, I gave her a copy to keep. I felt I had to explain to her that her name appeared as Foteini, when her real name is actually Eleni, not that she could read a word of English. All the same, I said I did it to give her anonymity and privacy, imagining this would be her choice because at heart she was an innocent character. She had never, she told me, been out of southern Greece and only had a vague idea where Britain was, despite the maps I'd drawn for her in the dust. I had decided to change her name when we were back in Scotland for a time in 2013, when I was finishing edits on the book before publication.

It wasn't until 2014, when we returned to Greece and I gave her a copy of *Feta*, that I explained the name change. I thought she'd nod with approval. Not a bit of it! She glared at me uncomprehending, sweeping her big calloused hand over the cover.

"Why would you call me Foteini? I don't like Foteini!" she grizzled loudly. "Why couldn't I be Eleni? I like my own name. Everyone here knows Eleni, not Foteini!"

I was stunned. Was this the woman I imagined was shy, who didn't like too much fuss? And then she shocked me further by appearing to be fine also with international recognition. Who knew? When I told her that readers from all over the globe had written to tell me how much they liked her, she beamed with joy. I had got it all wrong, obviously. She didn't rate the notion of 'anonymity'. "What's that, Margarita?" It's another Greek word, of course, *anonimia*, but as I'd discovered already, the Greeks have a different and refreshing sense of privacy. They don't covet it as we do and get petulant when other people invade it – up to a point. But in the end, true to her generous nature, Foteini accepted the name change.

And she didn't mind any of the attention that came her way. So, wrong on that score as well. Quite a few readers who contacted me via our website, after we'd returned to the UK for good in 2015, told me they'd gone to Megali Mantineia after reading *Feta*, to see what it was like and to scope out Foteini. Few of them actually found the farm compound, but many saw her on the road, riding Riko, and some sent me photos of the encounters. One reader waylaid her on the village road, gabbling on in beginner's Greek and waving a copy of *Feta*, shouting my name. They later told me that had made Foteini smile – and the anecdote did the same for me. These were wonderful stories to cherish. I hope the encounters gave her as much pleasure.

However, one couple – the wife was English and her husband was Greek, but he had been living in the UK for many years – were lucky enough to find Foteini at her farm and later wrote to tell me about it. It's one of my favourite Foteini stories.

They were touring the Mani on their way to a chic hotel on the restored Byzantine island of Monemvasia, in eastern Peloponnese. They detoured to see Megali Mantineia and find Foteini, which they did. Helped by the fact the husband spoke Greek, she invited them into the farm for coffee. They were shocked by the mess of stuff lying around: goats, cats and the distressed plastic table and chairs under the mulberry tree, the makeshift sink and water spout. It wasn't enticing to the uninitiated and this couple were dressed in smart clothes for their hotel stay.

The wife explained, "There I was in a spotless pair of white jeans sitting on a grimy chair drinking a cup of coffee, and water [always served in Greece with coffee] out of an old jam jar that Foteini had found in her shed after raking about in a cupboard. It was all she had for a glass container, she said, but when she first brought it out it was filled with rusty nuts and bolts, which she emptied onto the ground and quickly rinsed the jar under the outside tap. She then filled it up with water and put it beside my coffee cup. I don't think I dared take more than a few sips."

But they were thrilled to meet her – and the wife survived the encounter.

Foteini was usually quite neat and tidy when it came to serving coffee at her farm. However, she also offered us food stored in the shed. She had biscuits in plastic bags dropped off by well-meaning villagers, which never looked particularly appetising, and there was the small matter of the mice, which she'd already told me about. One day she handed us sealed packets containing a slice of cake, such as you buy in supermarkets or *periptera*, kiosks, as a snack. She cajoled us into trying the cake. It wasn't bad, if a little tasteless and dry. I asked her where she she'd bought the packets.

"Oh, there was a feast day in a nearby village the other day and some gypsy girls were there handing out these little cakes. Good, eh?"

Jim and I looked at each other and I discretely checked the use-by dates on the packets, as I felt sure no-one else would have bothered. They were slightly old, but we survived.

Since we returned to the UK, I have sadly had little contact with Foteini, apart from letters I've written, to which she has always replied, in big, scrawled writing, always full of warm greetings. I've also called her at her village house, which has a phone at least, but which she rarely hears ringing because she's going deaf. But when she finally picks up the phone, I always feel a stab of nostalgia. I hear motor scooters backfiring on the road nearby, donkeys braying, and Foteini shouting over the lot of it, asking when we're going to return to the village to buy a house, and stay forever.

Then I have to explain, as I have many times, why we can't come back for good, or even for the long odyssey of the past. I always promise her a short visit the next time we're in southern Greece. Still, her usual refrain is, "You've forgotten me now."

"How could I ever forget you?" is always my response. And she guffaws loudly at that.

And how could I? I always remember that early in our stay in Greece she said to me, without any sense of boasting, "You know, Margarita, there isn't anyone else here quite like me."

Of course, there isn't. There isn't anyone else on the planet quite like Foteini. And it was my great good fortune to discover that.

2

All steamed up in Messinia

A COUPLE of years ago, while we were back in Britain, I wrote to a Greek friend to tell her we would be spending a month in the southern Peloponnese at the end of summer.

"Come and stay at the taverna," Maria said. "Yiorgos won't be there, he'll be in Athens with me, and our apartment above the taverna will be empty for a month."

Yiorgos runs the Ayia Playia taverna in Falanthi, a quiet, remote village north of Koroni, at the bottom of the Messinian peninsula. He's a popular figure in the area and works hard most of the year in his business and helps with olive harvesting in the winter. But sometimes, at the end of the summer, he will shut the taverna to spend time with his wife and small son, who live in Athens, four hours' drive away. This is a circumstance common in Greece where couples are often forced to live apart because of job commitments, and this was especially true during the economic crisis. But in this instance, Maria has a senior government position and needs to be in the capital, whereas Yiorgos has to spend most of the year in Falanthi.

"The taverna will be locked up, but our cook Meropi will come every day to feed the dog and do a few little chores about the place, so you won't have to worry about a thing. Just relax and have a nice time," said Maria.

It was a kind and generous offer from a woman I had always admired, but we know from having lived in Greece that when someone says you won't have to worry about a thing, it doesn't always go that way. Greece is a place of maddening but intoxicating spontaneity, where rules and routines are bendy things. And having seen inside many rural homes, but not this apartment, I didn't know what to expect. Greek houses can be as eccentric as the people: post-war kitchens, toilets that don't work properly, roofs that leak, windows that never shut, pipes that growl and rattle. But I had faith that judging by the taverna and the couple themselves this would be a fully functioning apartment.

We arrived at the taverna on the appointed day, just as Yiorgos was packing for Athens, much later than he should have been because like most Greeks he likes to do things with a bit of brinkmanship, at the last minute, chivvied along by Meropi. Once he'd gone, and for the first day or so, it seemed strange to find ourselves in a friend's home for the first time when they weren't there. It seemed slightly voyeuristic, but the place was comfortable and everything seemed to work, especially the kitchen. Maria had left us bottles of fresh bright green olive oil and bags of heady, dried oregano and basil, local honey and home-made jam, with a note telling us to help ourselves to everything.

The house had a long veranda on one side with hillside views, a small table and several chairs, where we could have our breakfast in the sun – except for the mornings when the ubiquitous cats of Greece decided to call by and spread themselves out on the furniture, or in the plant pots, in the usual fashion, sometimes bringing you an offering of field mice, frogs and so forth. The yard was typically ramshackle: a vegetable patch where large mutant courgettes were scarpering off in every direction, and a clapped-out car showing a thin attempt to use it as a makeshift greenhouse for growing tomatoes.

The views over the yard to distant hills were entrancing. The taverna had a spring water outlet in the front paved courtyard, pouring cold mountain water into a carved marble basin below. Yiorgos told us this had been the main water supply for the village in past centuries and though there was now a proper water supply, locals still liked to fill up their plastic bottles here.

Meropi, the cook/caretaker/overseer, was a charming woman, with smiley, pale brown eyes, who gave a sense instantly that while she was genial, she wouldn't stand any kind of nonsense. What exactly she'd been told about our stay was probably sketchy. Details of how long, what we would be doing and other imponderables would, I imagined, not have been covered. In Greece, no-one ever gets a whole story. You learn to read minds, simple as that.

She came every day to check the taverna and feed the big brown dog, Iraklis (Hercules), kept in a fenced part of the yard. She was also apparently tasked with doing an autumnal clean-up, laundering all the linen in the taverna: tablecloths, napkins and so forth. She explained she would need to come up to the apartment every day to use the washing machine, installed in the family bathroom, but she would iron downstairs if we preferred.

"You can iron up here if you like," I said, thinking of the big empty taverna below and that we'd be out all day. Anyway, I assumed when I made the offer that she'd pass on it to be polite.

"Oh, could I? That's so kind of you, *efharisto poli*," she said, thanking us, her eyes dancing with delight. My stomach twitched with uncertainty for an unaccountable reason. But it was too late to renege on the offer. And I could tell how much she liked being up in the three-bedroom apartment, how homely and quiet it must have seemed, as she lived in a small village house not far from a busy road.

She had her own key and said she would come and go quietly after we were up in the morning. She was polite and always waited until she sensed signs of life above the taverna before tapping at the front door, arms full of dirty washing for the machine. This was her strategy for the first few days, with the washing strung up afterwards on the balcony to dry and brought down early the next day – if the cats hadn't climbed up first and unpegged it. Then the ironing would begin (tablecloths mostly) and it was clear that Meropi, unlike most Greeks I'd ever met, liked to have a strict schedule. It was the thing I'd sensed in her eyes when we first met – unwavering domestic urgency, but softened by politeness.

She liked to have the ironing board set up in front of the TV, watching one of the many Greek soaps that always sounded to my ear like British pantomimes, loud and hyperbolic with hysterical characters. She'd labour amiably amid the pungent hiss of the steam iron, one eye on the TV screen, seemingly unfazed by the sight of us ferrying breakfast backwards and forwards to the balcony, or noisily gathering up our kit and beach supplies for the day. It was a curious set-up but it was useful to have someone to chatter to in Greek and improve my rusty skills after a couple of years back in Britain. For her part, she could multi-task seamlessly with domestic chores and Greek instruction without breaking a sweat.

For the first few days this 'holiday routine' breezed along like life on a steam setting. I didn't see a problem because how long would tablecloths take anyway? It was a rural taverna, not the Dorchester! A week and it would all be done and dusted and the place would be ours. But by the second week, the piles of tablecloths kept coming until they were overtaken by linen serviettes, seemingly hundreds of them. Okay, Jim and I reasoned, a week of serviettes, how bad could that be? And by the end of the second week, we were now chilled-out after long days of sun and sea. We were in holiday mode, nonchalant about things like housework – anyone's housework.

Once or twice we slept in and Meropi would turn up at the front door looking flustered, her arms full of more fodder for the washing machine and the inevitable pile of ironing to be done. Only occasionally did our tardiness make her a little fractious, but like most Greeks she was easily mollified with a breezy chat or with the wrapped sweets we'd brought from the UK that I often left for her on top of her ironed-and-folded pile on a chair, which she removed only when the stack reached giddying heights. At least once the schedule went all to hell when we returned from the beach tired from swimming, just before siesta time, and decided on a nap, as Meropi had usually gone by then. On the edge of sleep, I heard the front door opening and footsteps in the sitting room. I sat up in bed panicking, thinking we were about to be burgled. Then the washing machine started up and I realised it could only be Meropi, working later than usual or, failing that, it was a pernickety rural bandit with a taste for washing the linen before he stole it.

What had seemed a peculiar routine at the beginning started to feel almost normal: the washing, ironing, the loud

Greek TV soaps, the morning bustle. I even felt a sense of guilt that this sweet-natured woman – whom I learnt had put her daughter through university with all her hard, relentless work – was now having all her long-standing rituals toyed with by two *xenoi*, foreigners, living the life of Riley. But we had learnt from our time in Greece that this is a country where it's easy to fall into new or even crazy ways of life without missing a beat, as long as you leave all your ingrained preconceptions at the front door, along with the dusty sandals and the gang of scabrous cats.

Yet it was a beguiling month, with the taverna remote from nearby villages and only a few houses nearby. Yiorgos's rural neighbours seemed puzzled by our residency but kindly invited us to church services in the nearby tiny chapel and to feast day meals, probably to plunder us for explanations. The local *papas* (priest), Theodoros, seemed delighted to have a few more folk to bulk up the late summer congregation and one evening rang to invite us to a special celebration the following Sunday morning, after which we were invited back to his spartan but cosy village house in Homatero for lunch with his wife. It was a charming house, with many ecclesiastical touches and one wall covered in his hobby paintings, which were curious, sometimes bizarre depictions of both Greek life and portraits of well-known characters, like Einstein with more than the usual crazy hair, and slightly risqué images as well. Clearly, he had artistic talent and a wicked sense of humour, a world away from the Byzantine formality of his church services.

By the middle of the third week, Meropi was still toiling away over linens, which were about to be superseded by the taverna's curtains, long and thick, in preparation for cold winter nights ahead. Our hopes that the ironing marathon would end soon were now fading. But we had rituals of our own to cling to and by late afternoon, when a fresh breeze toyed with the plane trees over the front terrace, we got into the habit of decamping there with coffee, or perhaps a carafe of chilled wine. It was pleasant to do nothing but listen to the susurrus of wind and the trickle of water in the nearby stream that ran under a narrow stone bridge. It was like Brigadoon, without the tartan and the singing.

While Falanthi seems like a forgotten corner of Messinia, it had once been a hive of industry, with a lignite mine close to the taverna, which produced huge amounts of the brown coal from 1916 to the 1940s. It brought some prosperity to the area until the invading Germans arrived and closed it down and also raided the nearby village of Homatero, which was the local headquarters of the *andartes*, the rebel resistance group that fought against the Nazis. The rebels were captured and sent to Tripoli to be executed.

A two-storey house that is now the taverna and apartment above was bought by the grandfather of Yiorgos in the early 20th century and Yiorgos has run the business for more than 30 years.

One afternoon we were sitting on the front terrace, quietly drinking wine and reading books. A car pulled up and a middle-aged couple got out and ambled towards us, admiring the terrace and its surroundings.

"This is so cute, isn't it, Theo?" said the woman loudly. I picked up an Aussie accent. She had thick blonde hair and was wearing a long floaty summer dress, a clash of chunky beads around her neck.

"Sure is, darl. But is the taverna open?" the man asked, addressing the question more to us.

"Afraid not," said Jim. "It won't open until November."

"Oh, jeez! Whatdya think of that?" said the woman, nudging Theo's upper arm.

"We've swung by just to have a meal here. A friend in Finicounda recommended it. So that's a god-damned nuisance and we're leaving in a couple of days," said Theo, with a slight whine in his voice, looking hot and harassed. He wiped his forehead with a crumpled handkerchief.

Jim and I looked at each other. One of Jim's eyebrows flickered with amusement.

"Couldn't you open it just this once, just for a simple meal? No trouble, you understand. Geez, we're starving," said the wife, with a pleading look in her big blue eyes.

"I wish we could but it's not our taverna," I said, wondering how they imagined that two foreigners would be running a traditional place like this in the middle of nowhere.

"Oh, I see. So ... you're just ... what ... minding the shop?" the woman asked.

"And the owners?" asked Theo.

"In Athens. We're staying in the couple's apartment above for the month, that's all. We're old friends."

Theo nodded, his mouth puckering with disappointment.

"I'm Denise, by the way," his wife said, reaching towards us for a handshake. "Sorry for trying to put you on the spot like this."

"Don't worry about it. Are you Aussies, by the way?" I asked, suddenly remembering how comically forthright they could be at times.

"Yeah, but how'd you guess that?" Theo said with playful sarcasm in his broad 'ocker' accent. He looked more relaxed now "I'm an inner-city Greek Aussie from Sydney, but Denise is fair dinkum Australian, aren't you, darl."

I smiled. It was a while since I'd heard a proper Aussie accent. I could appreciate the Greekness now in Theo's wiry dark hair and in his large Levantine eyes.

"Sit down for a minute if you like," said Jim, nodding towards the other two chairs at the table. "Would you like some wine at least. We've got plenty."

"Raiding the taverna, eh? Thanks, don't mind if we do. And we'll drink whatever you're having," said Theo.

While they got settled, Jim nipped upstairs for a couple more of the squat glasses favoured in Greece, and another carafe of white wine. We had built up decent stocks of wine and food, because there were no nearby stores to nip out to. While it was tempting, we didn't want to raid the taverna for booze, even though we had the run of the place when Meropi wasn't there. We had our own keys to the taverna and were tasked with checking on it every night to make sure all was well, the doors were firmly locked, lights out, and Iraklis the dog had been fed and hadn't decided to leg it over the fence – yet!

When their wine was poured and a bowl of pistachio nuts set down on the table, Theo explained that his father's family came from Finicounda, on the west of the peninsula, while his mother hailed from Kalamata.

"My father still owns a house in Fini, a bit of a shit old place now, but we always stay in it when we come over. My uncle in Fini keeps an eye on it for us the rest of the time. We come over every few years or so. We always say we'll spend a long summer here one time and fix the house up a bit, but we haven't so far. Work and family commitments and all that. Never stopped by this taverna before though. But, hey, six miles away and it's another world in Greece, isn't it?"

Denise nodded, sipped her wine and shelled pistachios with a famished, fumbling energy, half the nuts and shells pinging away on to the terrace.

"Jeez, it's lovely here though, isn't it, darl?" said Theo, looking up at the tall plane trees. But Denise didn't answer, preoccupied with her nuts.

"My Fini friend Panayiotis says he loves coming here. He says the owner does the best *kontosouvli* around, the proper spit-roasted pork, and there's nothing like it," he said, licking his lips. "Panayiotis didn't mention that the place might be shut. I'll have to rouse him over that. Sorry, reprimand him."

Theo didn't spot my own Aussie accent. After all the years away it's a mild 'twang' now, as most people describe it, and an accent that seems to have plucked influences from the different places I've lived. He was surprised when

I told him I'd grown up in the southern suburbs of Sydney and that Jim and I had worked in Sydney for some years. I then offered a potted history of our relationship with Greece.

"Oh, man! We'd love to do what you guys did with the Greek odyssey. Wouldn't we, darl? Just cut loose, go a bit bush for a while and spend a year or so in Fini, and learn to speak better Greek."

"Why don't you?" I said, realising that close up they were probably in their late fifties, and Theo maybe a bit older. Just right for a midlife adventure.

Denise sipped her wine and rolled her eyes. I got the sense she'd heard this proposition of Theo's many times before.

"Sometimes you just can't step away from your life that easily, Theo, you know that. I mean, it sounds easy, but not when you've got kids and ageing parents and all that," she said.

"Well, the kids are big now, they're not ankle biters, and the oldies are well set up in their retirement bungalow," he said, addressing the doubting Denise before turning to us. "The thing is, guys, I'm retiring next year, more or less. I'm an accountant. Have my own business. I've made a good living. I'd like to hand it over to my eldest son and just do a bit of part-time consultancy work when I need to. You'd like that, darl. Go on, admit it. We can't spend all our lives working flat out like lizards drinking."

I laughed at the Aussie expression I hadn't heard for years.

Denise laughed too but there was more caution in her eyes.

I thought of our own adventure in 2010, when we'd packed in our jobs, rented out our apartment and left, with no idea if we'd ever work full-time again and not caring one way or the other. That's the point of adventure. You don't know what the consequences will be. It's meant to be that way, or it's not adventure.

"You've got a house to live in at least, in Fini. We had to rent the whole time we were here, and that wasn't always easy," I said.

"That's true, we're lucky to have the old house, but believe me it will need a load of hard yakka to get it up to scratch," said Denise, polishing off the last of the nuts.

We spent an hour or so drinking and chatting about midlife adventures. They were an entertaining couple, down to earth, amusing.

"Is there anywhere else around here we could go for a meal tonight without going into villages on the road to Koroni?" asked famished Denise.

"There's a *kafeneio* in Homatero nearby, but they have only limited food."

They both pouted and we felt sorry for them.

"Look, we could sort something for you," said Jim.

Theo laughed. "Don't tell me you're going to fire up the taverna kitchen and cook us a meal? You devils!" he said, guffawing.

Denise had perked up a bit at the idea of dinner.

"No, not that," said Jim, chortling merrily. "We've got a kitchen upstairs. I made moussaka earlier and all I need to do is whack it back in the oven for a bit. That was our plan anyway. There would be plenty for four, with a small salad, if you like."

Jim has always liked cooking and moussaka is his favourite Greek dish. When we lived in the Mani for the first three years, we tried just about every taverna's moussaka for miles around, pestered taverna owners to learn their secrets, rated the moussakas secretly and Jim had even written a mad blog post about it.

"That would be awesome, guys, thanks. Whatdya say, darl?"

"Oh yeah, the moussaka would be welcome, but we don't want to put you two out."

"No trouble," said Jim.

Denise smiled vibrantly, showing off big, perfect teeth. She suddenly looked about 10 years younger.

We left them for a while and went upstairs to warm up the moussaka while I whipped up a quick Greek salad with feta cheese and tomatoes and peppers from Yiorgos's garden, a basket of fresh bread and another large carafe of wine.

It was a pleasant evening, still warm, and we set candles on the outside table. There was a lot of talk and laughter and several cars passing by slowed down in front of the taverna to peer at our dinner party. One old guy in a black cap came by, riding a donkey side saddle. He stopped and waved his stick at us, asking if Yiorgos had come back. Was the taverna open? We told him no. Even in the half-light I could see his face droop with disappointment as he drummed his feet on the donkey's side and continued on his way.

"You know, you two could have opened the taverna this month and served a few dishes, if Jim's moussaka is anything to go by," said Theo, polishing off the final slice.

"Nice idea, Theo, but somehow I don't think so," I said, with a vision in my mind of us toiling away in the kitchen, with Meropi in charge no doubt, her orderly mind rattling over more than precision creases in tablecloths and napkins. It would either have been great fun, or hellish, with everything that could go wrong going spectacularly awry and Greek diners moaning like the north wind, as they often do in tavernas when food isn't quite to their liking. They'd be speed-dialling Yiorgos to plead for his return.

We finished up a few hours later after what had been a great evening, only marred slightly by Theo insisting that he pay us something for the meal, which we strenuously declined.

"Next time you're here in Messinia you can buy us a meal," Jim said.

"That's a deal then," said Theo vibrantly, shaking our hands. "And you know what? You two guys have inspired me now. I'm going to go back to Oz to make a plan to definitely come back here next summer, or the one after."

Denise made a comical face. Theo held out his arms and shrugged in the Greek way.

"What's that look for, darl? You'll see. This time I'm really going to go for it. I'm coming back here and I'll finally get that village house spruced up, something to leave to the kids anyway, their bit of Greek heritage. I mean, it was sheer luck, wasn't it, meeting these two guys here of all places, the taverna being shut, and this meal. Destiny, wasn't it, darl?" he said, sending her off into loud giggles.

We made them coffee before they left and said goodnight by the roadside. Theo hugged us both and thanked us for our 'wonderful *filoxenia*' (hospitality), which seemed amusing, as if we'd just twitched our noses and morphed into Greeks.

Theo wagged his finger at us. "You'll see, guys. One day. And we'll meet up again. In this taverna, us, part-time residents in the old homeland, eh?"

Denise rubbed Theo affectionately on the back, as if humouring him, the Greek husband after a few drinks getting nostalgic, maybe even teary sometimes, over his Greek roots and a dilapidated pile in the ancestral village luring him towards it like a Siren on a rock.

We exchanged email addresses and Theo promised to keep in touch and update us on his proposed odyssey.

The next morning, after sleeping in late, we found Meropi already setting up her ironing board. For once the sight of it made me feel mortally tired. She looked askance at us as we shuffled across the sitting room, sleepy-eyed, carrying bowls of cereal to the balcony.

"Someone must have called by the taverna this morning," she said, "and left those bottles for you outside."

She pointed to the dining table. Inside a plastic bag, there were four bottles of wine: two white and two Nemea red, one of the best labels in the Peloponnese. A card was taped to one bottle.

"Thanks for dinner. Great food, even better company. See you next year in Messinia. Love Theo and Denise xx"

I could tell that Meropi was eager for an explanation, and no doubt had already heard gossip from the neighbours about the 'party' at the taverna, the table of foreigners, drinking till late, as if the taverna was re-opening. But suddenly a TV soap was starting with a blare of Turkish-sounding music and her attention was zapped towards the screen, so we flitted outside.

"That was kind. They must have left the bottles in front of the locked gate this morning," I said to Jim as we sat outside in the sun, eating breakfast. Only in Greece could you leave a gift in plain view of the road outside and find it was still there hours later. More amazing was the fact the couple had even managed to organise it long before we'd got out of bed.

By the time our holiday was nearly at an end, the rituals of life at the taverna, that had at first seemed odd, now seemed completely normal. Who doesn't get up in the morning to find a stranger in their sitting room ironing frantically, as if it were about to become a new Olympic sport?

A few days before we left, the ironing routine ceased but there was more industry in the taverna below. Just when I thought there couldn't be one thread left to wash and iron within a 100-mile radius of the taverna, out came Greek embroideries and wall hangings of indeterminate provenance that were draped over taverna tables, awaiting some needlework maintenance, or so Meropi explained.

One day after a trip to the beach, we passed the taverna windows on the way to the back stairs up to the apartment. We could see Meropi inside, labouring over folky embroidery. A small TV was blaring nearby, the usual cacophony from a diverting soap. Of course the embroideries and so forth were later ironed as well. However, it all took place downstairs this time, as if even Meropi knew when a good thing had been pushed far enough.

I thought I might miss her when we returned to England, and indeed I did, as I always miss everything about Greece: the good, the bad and, quite frankly, the bonkers! For a day or two, it was strange to walk through our sitting room in the morning and not hear the hiss of an iron and the hysterical blathering of Greek TV.

For the next two years, we didn't go back to Messinia, but occasionally we got an email from Theo telling us his exit plan was still 'a goer', the details always being tweaked. But I think I knew deep down, as Denise did, it wouldn't happen, not for years anyway, probably not ever. What you plan to do on a night of mad possibilities on a Greek terrace, after a few wines, can evaporate the next day like a coastal mist in the first shaft of sunlight. Or indeed like the mist from a steam iron in a manic race to clean all the restaurant linen in the whole of the southern Peloponnese!

3

Hugged by an octopus

A ROW of octopuses pegged on a line, like washing. It's one of the most memorable, and certainly quirky, images that tourists remember from Greece. But it no longer seems cute to me, nor is the idea of eating grilled octopus, even when it's perfectly cooked and doesn't have the texture of a swim flipper. One summer morning in southern Greece made me see the octopus in a very different light.

In all the years I've been going to Greece, I'd never seen a live octopus in the sea, even though I'm an avid swimmer and snorkeller and have ventured into the appropriate places: the calm, rocky outcrops where they usually like to build their lairs. However, a couple of years ago Jim and I were on a long summer break in the town of Koroni, Messinia. We were on a remote beach just north of the town, a favourite location when we'd lived there. While in the water, our attention was jagged by a German family wearing snorkelling gear. One of the kids was shouting about something he'd seen.

We looked over with interest at the group swimming near us in the warm, clear water. A moment later, the father dived in and the rest of the family gathered in a circle, floating on their stomachs, holding hands as if in a watery séance. It had now piqued our curiosity, so we swam over to have a look and luckily we were wearing swim goggles. The German guy surfaced. He was friendly and spoke English. He pointed out a curious arrangement of stones on the sandy bottom in about five feet of water.

"An octopus house," he said.

We put our faces in the water. The 'house' didn't look like much: one large flat stone and a few smaller ones set across a small gap and, comically, a bent stick wedged across the whole set-up like a front gate.

"Where's the octopus?" we asked the guy, who it turned out had a holiday home nearby and was familiar with the beach, having swum there for years, and familiar with octopuses, too.

"It's hiding under the rock. Give it a moment. It will come out," he said, putting his foot on the sand right next to the entrance to the lair. By now his kids had skittered off, bored, and it was just the three of us, staring down at the lair, willing the octopus to come out. After a while there was movement – the tip of a tentacle groped its way out, then more of it, until it was tickling one side of the guy's ankle. Then another tentacle appeared and finally out popped the whole octopus. It was small, a young one perhaps, and dark brown. The guy seemed pretty relaxed about things, even when two tentacles fastened themselves round either side of his ankle in a strange watery hug.

"He's pulling me!" he said excitedly. "He's really strong. He's trying to pull me towards his house!"

He wasn't kidding. We could see the tentacles drawing tight, the body edging backwards. Was he just playing with the man, or did he fancy having him for lunch, a humorous reversal in a country where barbecued octopus is always on the menu? The pulling went on a while and then, finally, the creature gave up, and slithered back under the rock.

It was a pretty amazing spectacle, and back on the beach we chatted with the German guy for a while about octopuses. He was a keen underwater amateur photographer as well, and it wasn't his first experience of being hugged by this octopus. He'd already taken video footage of his encounters.

We went back to the beach the next day, hoping to see the holidaymaker again and watch another man/octopus interface, but as fate would have it, he never reappeared and must have returned home. His parting gift to us, however, had been the amazing introduction to this curious little creature we named Oscar. And we were left with the challenge of trying to lure him out ourselves for a hug. Strange obsessions can grow on long indolent holidays when the imagination is given a long rein.

With the October weather being exceptionally good, we went back for the next few days, and easily located Oscar's lair. Jim would set about replicating the German's stance next to the 'doorway', keeping his foot planted firmly in the sand. While I was desperate to do the same, I was too short to keep my foot steady on the sea bottom without drowning! Even for Jim, it proved harder than we thought because even mild currents made it difficult to hold steady in one place for long, so I had to add extra weight to Jim's efforts by leaning hard on his shoulders to keep him steady. I imagine this made us look peculiar, like a watery art installation mounted for the entertainment of other holidaymakers and we drew some very strange glances. Nevertheless, we tried out this routine for a few days but Oscar didn't want to come out, even though we could see he was curled up inside the lair, often one eye visible at the doorway, guarding his turf. Perhaps he didn't trust us and had become accustomed only to the German and his leg offering.

"Never mind, we've got plenty of days to go yet. Sooner or later, we'll get lucky, you wait and see!" said Jim valiantly.

We had never really thought much about octopuses until we read a new book, ironically, just before we'd left for this Greek holiday. Called *Other Minds: The Octopus and the Evolution of Intelligent Life,* by Peter Godfrey-Smith, it was full of curious anecdotes that shed light on this amazing creature that has the intelligence roughly of a dog or a three-year-old child – and the mischief to match.

The octopus is a cephalopod related to squid and cuttlefish that developed from a snail-like creature about 290 million years ago. It compensated for losing its shell by developing a large brain. They are capable of playing and recognising different humans. They can even 'see' through their skin. Godfrey-Smith believes they are the "closest we will come to meeting an intelligent alien".

Octopuses inspired the imagination of mankind long before we understood much about them. The ancient Greek philosopher Aristotle wrote about them and they were admired also by the Byzantine Greeks, who feature them in many of their old church frescos, especially the *Ainoi* (the Praises), an image which always depicts Christ encircled by the sun and moon and various creatures from elephants to scorpions – and octopuses. We had seen one Byzantine fresco in a monastery near Koroni featuring an impish-looking octopus.

Octopuses are not only smart, they're also adept at interacting with humans, as we'd seen in a small way with the German tourist. In a study at the University of Otago in New Zealand, where octopuses were kept in laboratory tanks, researchers discovered the creatures could turn off the lights (they don't like bright light) by squirting jets of water at the overhead light bulbs when no-one was watching, short-circuiting the power supply.

Godfrey-Smith, a philosopher of science and a keen scuba diver, has done much of his own investigation of octopus behaviour and revealed they are keen to interact, to touch nearby humans, as we had already seen with the German tourist.

The writer said, "If you sit in front of their den and reach out a hand, they'll often send out an arm or two, first to explore you, and then – absurdly – to try to haul you into their lair."

After nearly a week of excursions to the beach on Oscar patrol, during which there had been some cloudy, windy weather with poor water visibility, we had to give up for a bit but continued when the weather improved. Curiously, the lair had been undisturbed by the unsettled weather and we found Oscar still inside, the front gate still in place and a gimlet eye near the opening. And Oscar seemed more responsive this time to Jim's efforts to connect. Maybe it was a case of finally putting a name to a foot. With our heads just in the water, watching through our goggles, we were finally rewarded with the sight of one tentacle slowly groping its way to Jim's ankle and attaching itself, and then another tentacle round the other side. Then, as before, Oscar moved completely out of his lair and stood beside Jim's foot, the two tentacles straining, the others locked into position behind him.

Jim ducked his head out of the water. "He's pulling my foot! My God, it feels weird! He's really strong," said Jim, with an edge of hysteria in his voice. "I hope he doesn't pull me into the den!"

"In your dreams, Jim. You wouldn't fit!" I sniped, because I had octopus-hug envy really bad. Why couldn't it be me too, I thought? It would have been right up there with swimming with dolphins or snorkelling with whales.

We stood in the water until our hands were getting pruney and other bathers were probably beginning to think we were bonkers, staring at the seabed for far too long. After a while, Oscar got bored with trying to lug a goliath into his house and slithered back inside, watching us all the while with the one eye at the front door. Although we returned for a few more days, and went through the same 'foot' routine several more times, Oscar never emerged again. Low boredom threshold perhaps. Game over!

"He did it once, just to shut us up, that's all," I said to Jim, disappointed at his single encounter with the brainy beastie.

Or maybe Oscar had a sense of humour as well as brains. It was a bit of a tease, and a payback for all the cephalopods we'd ever eaten, which get hauled out of the Greek sea by their thousands every year to satisfy tourists' appetites. I shuddered when I thought of the many times we'd seen a fisherman with a freshly caught octopus, bashing it on rocks, apparently to tenderise it before it was hung on a 'washing line' in the sun to dry, ready to be chargrilled.

One night, not long after the Oscar hug, we were having dinner with a Greek couple, Eleni and Tasos, who had been our neighbours when we lived on a Koroni hillside a few years earlier. Tasos is a genial guy who likes a good wind-up and having been a fisherman early on in life, he was very interested when we told him our octopus story.

"You were lucky to find one. They're quite rare in these parts now. The eggs get eaten by some African fish that's breeding now in these waters. If you tell any other Greeks where you saw the octopus exactly, they'll go out and catch it, so don't say a word. Okay?"

We nodded, horrified.

"But you can tell me," he said with a wink. "Just out of interest."

"Ho, ho. No way!" I told him.

"But it was the beach below the church of the Panayia, yes?"

"Could be. But it's a long beach, as you know," I said primly, trying to put him off. If anyone could find Oscar, I guessed Tasos might if he'd had a mind to.

Before our Oscar encounter, we too had loved eating barbecued octopus, the particular way it's done in Greece. However, after our experience on the beach neither of us wanted to eat it ever again. More so, when a week later we were shopping at a local *laiki* market by the sea and strolled past the fish counter. The sight of a lone, dead octopus lying on a metal tray stopped me in my tracks. It was on its side, one big dark eye staring, glossy, unblemished, as if it had been killed only moments earlier. It had a pitiful, accusatory stare and I had to look away quickly.

To this day neither Jim nor I have eaten octopus. You can't eat a species that's gone out of its way to hug you and invite you into its beach hut. I sense that when we next visit that beach in Messinia we will be looking for a new lair, set up perhaps by the progeny of Oscar – if our friend Tasos hasn't rumbled it first.

4

Secrets of Greek village life

NOT all Greek villages are created equally. Two villages can be a few miles apart, with roughly the same history and geographical aspect, yet one will be buzzing and the other will be dwindling into oblivion. And Greeks seem to have a kind of 'village rage' where they get in a strop over whose village is superior.

While on holiday in the Pelion region, on the mainland north of Athens, a few years back, we were strongly reminded of this when we wandered into an old-fashioned souvenir shop selling everything from embroidered wool slippers to snorkel sets and brass statues of naked Apollo. It was in the village of Milina, set on the gulf side of the Pelion peninsula, with a long sandy beach. The black-clad owner of a venerable age asked us where we were staying. I told her Metochi, in the foothills behind. She pulled a great lemony face.

"Metochi!" she croaked. "Why would you want to stay there? There's nothing there. Nothing but old houses. Pah! Here is better," she said, waving towards the vista of crowded tavernas and sun loungers along the beachfront.

I laughed at her put-down of Metochi for being the poor relation to the buzzy, thriving Milina. In her mind Metochi was a village in its death throes. The fact that we were staying there made her look at us with dark suspicion. I think she was even relieved when we left the shop, and she probably crossed herself too.

Jim and I had rented a villa in the south of the region for a month. Pelion is part of the Magnesia Prefecture, and is mainly one long peninsula shaped like a crab's claw with a huge mountainous region at its head tapering down to a thin curve of idyllic coves in the south. The villa was on the edge of Metochi, which was quiet, with not many inhabitants apparently, but gorgeous views towards the Pagasitikos gulf and well placed to access both this side of the peninsula and the other, on the Aegean, with the islands of Skiathos and Skopelos nearby.

In Metochi, there are several run-down and abandoned houses in the centre of the village and on the hillside behind, and it certainly wasn't hoaching with people that September. On the surface it was just a village on the way to somewhere else, as it's on the 'main' road from the thriving town of Argalasti to the bigger village of Lafkos further south, and then on down the peninsula to some very attractive coves. Lafkos, however, is a very pretty village with a large church and grand *plateia* (square) with classical houses and busy tavernas. It also has the oldest coffee shop in Greece. The Kafeneio Forlidas was established in 1785 and has been a magnet for locals and visitors ever since, including the acclaimed author Alexandros Papadiamandis, who spent a few weeks living in a room above the *kafeneio*, penning one of his masterpieces.

The *plateia* is usually the hub of a Greek village and always a good indication as to whether a village is thriving or not. Some of the more vibrant villages in the Pelion mountains further north have sumptuous squares, such as Makrinitsa, set under massive plane trees and with a view down to the city of Volos. But Makrinitsa is bigger, with a stronger foothold in the region's history.

Metochi's central hub was a 'ghost *plateia*', always near-deserted during the day, even though it had a big, airy aspect and views to the gulf. An old traditional *kafeneio* was shut indefinitely, with a notice pinned to the window announcing as much. The only time we saw people in the *plateia* was at night, and men mostly, drinking beer and playing the board game *tavli*, keeping a gimlet eye on any movement on the road below, as if wary of who was traversing their patch, and why.

At the top of a set of stone steps ascending from the road, a hand-painted sign had been fixed to the trunk of a plane tree, saying '*I plateia tou horiou mas*', our village square, which was a touching, yet forlorn message reaching across the years no doubt from happier days. The semi-abandonment of Metochi speaks of a village having lost its way at some point, apart from some modern, discreet holiday villas at its outskirts, surrounded by olive groves, like the house we were renting.

If there were people living near us, we rarely saw them, but when we did, the villagers were keen to chatter. One day, when I was closing the front gates for the evening, a middle-aged woman in black passed by and stopped. Typical of most rural Greeks, she wanted to know who I was, where from, how old, how long we were staying. We chatted a while and then she asked her final question: how much was the owner renting out his house for, because her daughter also had one to rent nearby, if we were interested? Cheeky! She said the last bit with a sly flicker of an eyebrow.

"Oh, I can't discuss that," I said firmly.

"Why ever not?" she asked, looking me up and down with a critical stare.

"It's not for me to discuss the owner's rental business. That wouldn't be right."

She said nothing more, apart from a hasty 'good evening' and she turned to leave with an upward toss of her chin.

The village had obviously had a different life once. At the northern end of Metochi there's a natural spring, spouting cool sweet water into a large marble bowl, where people still stop regularly to fill up bottles. Across the road from the spring, there's an abandoned taverna with a huge barbecue still visible through a large front window, for spit-roasting meat. The broad paved terrace out the front would have once been packed, especially on important feast days, but is now just an empty space where fallen leaves twirled in the wind like phantoms.

This is a reflection of what's happening everywhere in rural Greece. In the Mani we found hillside villages that were beautifully sited with once lovely stone houses that were now crumbling. In one village we found an abandoned taverna, its door hanging open and a collection of old junk and furniture piled up inside. In one corner was a box of old school books, lessons scrawled down the page. Either the owners couldn't be bothered to clear the place out when they left, or they left in one hell of a hurry, perhaps after an earthquake. It was a tableau I'd seen occasionally in earlier decades in Greece, though for different reasons, as most villages then were still thriving, and the punishing austerity of the recent economic crisis hadn't happened yet. But when an old taverna or *kafeneio*, in particular, was abandoned, often it had a compelling back story.

During a trip to Crete in the 1970s I was hitch-hiking around the island with a university friend from England. Patrick and I were on a long, early summer holiday with a limited budget. We arrived late one afternoon on the outskirts of Hania, on the north-west coast, and stopped at a long, deserted beach to eat the cheese pies we'd bought earlier at the port and drink a couple of beers. We had no accommodation booked for the night. Back then, it was easy to scramble rooms together. Those were the days when locals met boats arriving at the ports and held up makeshift signs indicating rooms to rent, usually in their own homes.

However, as we sat on the beach in the late afternoon sunshine, we were in no hurry to move. It was quiet, as it was in Crete in those days before mass tourism opened up the island and development began. We walked along the beach and came across a taverna, partially obscured from the road and the edge of a nearby village, by a row of thick tamarisk trees and oleander bushes. The taverna was a simple stone building with a faded sign over a scuffed blue door that read *Taverna Leventis*. It had a folky painting underneath of a tough-looking Cretan man in traditional clothes and black boots, riding a horse, which seemed to fit with the name of the taverna, *leventis* meaning a fearless or gallant man.

There were weathered, shuttered windows at the front of the taverna, but round the side one window had no shutters and we peered through grimy glass into a gloomy space beyond. We could just make out tables and rush-bottomed chairs. At the back was a kitchen area with small windows up near the ceiling. There was a grill for spit-roasting, a sink and on the counter in front were rows of bottles and a stack of plates, as if it were still in use. But the general state of the place implied it had been shut a long time.

Patrick ran his hand over the window. "Let's give this a shove and see if we can get a better look inside."

Patrick was Irish and he had a maverick soul. He liked to live on the edge, much more than I did, and during our holiday I often had to steer him away from risky situations. I was also intrigued by this shuttered old place and didn't see the harm in having a better look through an open window at least. The wood around the frame was badly weathered and when Patrick pushed firmly with the palm of his hand, the window gave way, the two sides of it swinging inwards with a loud crunch, and the sound of a handle falling to the floor. We peered in. A rancid, musty smell swirled towards us, sucked out through the open window. We both coughed, our eyes smarting. We stood a while at the window, trying to adjust our eyes to the dark interior. Patrick as usual was impatient.

"I'm going in. Might as well have a proper look inside. What do you say?"

"I don't know if that's such a good idea." Too late. He'd already heaved himself onto the window ledge and swung his legs inside.

While I was mulling over the wisdom of breaking and entering in a foreign country, Patrick made his way across the taverna to the front door, fiddling with the lock, muttering. Then I heard him retreating to the back of the taverna, trying what seemed to be another door. I heard it being wrenched open with a horrible noise like buckled wood dragged over scattered debris.

"Come on in!" he shouted. I made my way to the back of the taverna on a narrow path.

"The front door was locked. This one was too, but the key was left in the keyhole on the inside. It's as if the place is inviting us in," he said with a twinkle in his brown eyes.

I smiled. Patrick *would* see it that way. I followed him into the taverna, more to keep an eye on any further exploits he might be planning. He opened a few other windows and shutters to let in light and air, and I thought it was lucky for us it was still siesta time and there was no-one around to see what we were up to. Even with more light, it was a dismal, stuffy space that looked like one of those roped-off rooms you find in historic houses that tease you with a glimpse of the past but are essentially holding their secrets tight to their chest.

The taverna was a jumble of tables and chairs at odd angles, with some chairs overturned. On one table top was the board game *tavli*, still with the pieces in place, and two small empty wine glasses. An ancient *soba* (wood-burning stove) near one wall still had the charred remnants of wood inside. But the kitchen space at the back of the taverna was the most revealing: dirty plates stacked everywhere and piled up in the sink, with the congealed remains of food, picked at by myriad insects. On the serving counter lay an order book and a few pencils. We flicked through the book, which showed two months in summer, no year. With the rudimentary Greek I'd learnt in my work year in Athens, where I'd gone for an adventure after I left school in Sydney, I could make out the scrawl of different meals and drinks: moussaka, roast pork, salad, bread, retsina and raki. The prices were in drachma, the old currency.

"This is incredible. Look at this place, as if everyone just fled in a panic and left it like it was," Patrick said, rubbing his hand across his chin.

We mused over what might have driven the owner away, along with all the diners. Just a few years before our visit, Greece had rid itself of the pernicious military dictatorship that had ruled the country from 1967 to 1974. Yet there was still a sense of upheaval in parts of Greece and hardship, with people adjusting cautiously to their new freedoms or living with the aftermath of imprisonment and torture.

"It must have been something cataclysmic because they left wine up there," I said, pointing to a shelf running around the top of the walls, still packed with dusty wine bottles lying on their sides.

"Shall we try a bottle, a cheeky wee local red perhaps?" Patrick said, with the mischievous charm of the Irish.

"There's no way of getting up there. We'd need a ladder."

He eyed up the tables but they looked old and shoogly. Patrick didn't have the heart for leaping on them, though I'd seen him do worse in Greece after drinking too much ouzo.

"I wonder at the nearby villagers though, leaving all this wine and the place being unlocked ... well, more or less," he said with a rakish grin, glancing towards the forced window.

"Maybe the place has bad vibes."

We spent so much time poking around in the taverna, snooping inside drawers, checking out a gallery of old black and white photos, we didn't hear the group of men at the back door. A gabble of Greek and then they filed in, their feet thundering over the old floorboards. We must have looked startled, whereas the men looked fierce. They were tall, deeply tanned, with thick moustaches, dressed in the black trousers and long boots favoured by Cretan men. Their eyes flared at us. Here was trouble. Patrick and I exchanged looks.

"Leave it to me," he whispered. "I'll sort it out, don't worry."

I nodded, wondering if he could do blarney in Greek as well. The luck of the Irish.

One of the men, slightly younger, with thick black curly hair and an open face, spoke up first in passable English.

"You are foreigners, yes?"

"Irish," replied Patrick confidently. Pointing to me, he said, "Scottish/Australian." This made me smile, as if our nationalities would somehow excuse us for committing a felony.

I apologised in Greek for our intrusion, looking towards the rest of the group, who were glowering and talking loudly together like a burly Greek chorus in an impromptu theatre offering.

"How did you get inside here?" the curly-haired guy asked.

I let Patrick explain with typical flourish and a bending of truth, how we were innocently lured by the curious sight of the abandoned taverna and how, fortuitously, the back door had been unlocked but with a key on the inside. He flicked me a warning look, as if I was about to contradict the story. As if! The English speaker translated for the men who, judging by their still-fierce expressions, seemed to find this an unlikely explanation, that foreigners would have the temerity to do what they liked, even in Crete, a place I had come to view as a rather maverick stronghold of free spirits. But there are always rules, their rules.

"I hope you're not thinking of calling the police," said Patrick. The curly-haired Cretan, who we discovered was called Babis, translated the comment. There was more yammering. One tall, fierce looking guy made a windmill motion with his arm, the Greek sign for anything they don't like, or trust.

"No, we do not do that," Babis said. "We do not like the police."

"So, you're not annoyed with us for coming inside?"

"Yes, we are!" he said, with a disapproving lift of his thick eyebrows. Patrick and I exchanged worried looks.

"But we won't break you, I promise," said Babis. I think he meant 'bite' but he seemed to like the joke and chortled, which eased the tension. I felt myself relax a bit. The other men were becoming impatient, eager to check out the taverna. Babis joined them, touching things, opening cupboards, flipping through the order book, as we had done, and talking quickly and loudly between themselves in their vibrant, but difficult dialect.

This was obviously the first time these locals had been inside the taverna as well – lately, at any rate – which seemed incredible, considering the place was on the edge of the village.

"What happened here? Why has this place been abandoned like this?" I asked Babis.

He relayed a story that didn't surprise me at all, of how the place had been raided by the military police in 1972 during the years of the military dictatorship. Suddenly the other men stopped what they were doing, aware of what Babis was relating, even if they couldn't understand the English.

Babis told us the owner of the taverna, Lefteris, was a popular figure in the area and known for being daring at times and outspoken. He had already survived the civil war in Greece in the late 1940s, fighting on the side of the communists. He had managed to avoid trouble through most of the years of the dictatorship but later on he became less careful. Or like many supporters of the left and centre-left he just grew sick of the violence of the junta with its punishing restrictions and arrests.

One particular summer night, Lefteris had invited musicians to play, as he often did. They were doing a broad repertoire of Cretan folk music but also the rousing songs of Mikis Theodorakis, the now-famous composer of the film score for *Zorba The Greek*. His compositions were banned because of his well-known left-wing views. This was a time when the works of many writers, artists and musicians were prohibited. And anyone engaging with these works would be arrested.

The musical evening was vibrant, and a little rowdy at times, and perhaps on a tip-off from a junta informant, some military policemen arrived at the taverna. They disbanded the musicians and dragged Lefteris out of the taverna, along with several other men. An argument ensued. One man tried to escape down the beach and was shot in the back. All the men were bundled into a police wagon and taken to a prison in Heraklion and eventually sent off to island prisons, as was common during these years. They were never seen again.

"A big tragedy for this village," said Babis. "And Lefteris was a good man, and the others. The wives were left with children to support. Everyone was frightened and fearing more punishments to come. All the other people in the taverna that night, they just leave the place as it is and never come back – until *today*," he said, with emphasis. A funereal silence fell over the taverna. Patrick and I looked quickly at each other.

"That's a terrible story," Patrick said, looking unusually contrite.

In order to convey our sympathies to the others I quickly added in Greek, "My friend Patrick says this is a tragic story and we're very sorry for your losses here." The men nodded gravely, but said nothing.

I looked away, feeling uncomfortable. There was even more of an aura about the place now that we'd heard the story, and a sense of menace and chaos in the way the chairs and tables were scattered and overturned just as they had been in 1972 and everything else abandoned where it lay. The scene captured the essence of that terrifying night that must have started with so much hope, high spirits and music but was silenced in a few moments of senseless violence.

"So you never heard anything about the fate of the ones taken away?" I asked Babis.

He shook his head. "Only one was heard of. He went back to Athens, where he came from, a broken man, tortured, half-dead anyway and he later died. But the others, we heard only that they went to island prisons, but nothing more. They disappeared, like many people in those years, particularly the communists. If they signed statements to say they would give up their beliefs, they were set free. If not, they were tortured and killed. None of the men from here would sign the papers of the junta. Lefteris would never do it."

I suddenly felt bad, as if it were sacrilege to have blundered in here when we should have known better, when we should have guessed that something extraordinary had happened here. I felt it was time to leave.

Despite their former glowering looks, now that the whole story had been aired the men showed no sense of rancour. They carried on poking about the taverna, even bothering to right the chairs and tables, to gather up the order book and some of the photos. I had the strange impression watching them that they were probably relieved in some way that the place had been opened up. I shared my thoughts with Babis.

"You are right, my friend. No-one in the village wanted to come here during these past years, even the family of Lefteris. They feel bad, you know. And we Greeks are sus …" he stumbled over his English.

"Suspicious," I offered.

"Yes, thank you – especially about things to do with the death of those we know. We villagers have even feared coming here. But now the taverna is open, because of you both," he said, with a subtle nod of approval, or forgiveness perhaps, "we let the light in now, yes? And it is time to do something with this old taverna."

"Quite true, it's the best way to look at it," said Patrick, with his typical chipper take on things.

Babis explained to the others his notion of letting in the light at last and they seemed to agree with the sentiment, becoming suddenly more upbeat, less scary. I felt we had finally been exonerated from 'breaking in'. Two of the men even slapped us on the back and praised us for doing something they'd never wanted to do. One of them was eyeing up the wine. He said something to Babis.

"Yiannis here says we will take the wine. Lefteris would never want it to be wasted. We will share it round the village."

One man leapt up on a table, undeterred by creaking woodwork and reached out to one row of bottles. He seemed to know what he was looking for. He plucked out two of them and jumped back to the floor.

"For you," he said to Patrick. One was a bottle of red wine, the other a bottle of Cretan raki, the firewater so beloved of these stalwart people, who in their demeanour always reminded me of feisty Scottish highlanders.

Patrick took the bottles, brushing the dust off them to read the labels.

"Thank you. We'll be drinking to your health, my friends," he said.

I smiled, but my mind was spinning around the story we'd just heard and how incredible it was that this taverna had been left alone all this time, with no-one removing the wine. But I knew from experience of Greeks in those days that they were honest to a fault. There used to be a rather hackneyed joke passed around in the 1970s in Athens that if you dropped a 1,000 drachma note in the middle of Syntagma Square it would still be there later when you went back to retrieve it.

To show there were no hard feelings, the Cretan men gave us directions to a house with a few rooms to rent in the village and invited us to the local taverna in the village *plateia* for a meal and a drink to celebrate the 'opening' of the Leventis.

It was a long, happy, boozy evening, with someone playing a Cretan lyra and others dancing. It all necessitated another few days spent in the village, to get over mild hangovers, and it turned out to be the strangest experience of our summer holiday, if not the best.

Perhaps the *kafeneio* in Metochi had suffered a tragedy of its own. We would never know. But Metochi, with its abandoned *kafeneio,* had a similar ambience to many other villages I've encountered in Greece: it spoke of lives once well lived, of *parea*, company, *kefi*, high spirits, of celebrations and feast days, full of life, and occasionally tinged with tragedy.

The most abandoned of these villages in Greece serve as grave markers to the past, and to past catastrophes and secrets. Especially during the economic crisis, no-one had the money to revive them, no matter how much they wanted to. And they probably never would.

Greek villages are unique and a world apart, whether they buzz or not. But for outsiders who choose to live in them, navigating their cultural terrain and social networks often requires more of you than you sometimes want to give. But in the end they give you experiences and insights that are incomparable.

5

The woman who turned into a church

SOME of the strangest encounters we've had in Greece have been in connection with Greek Orthodox churches, especially old Byzantine ones. For this reason we developed a great interest in tracking down unusual churches, mainly because we would always find something there we didn't expect, or couldn't explain, such as a miraculous icon, a spooky atmosphere, or a strange and chilling back story.

In one rural church in the Mani, we saw a fresco of a saint with the bizarre addition of a terrifying second face, complete with long bloodied fangs, painted over his naked torso. Had the iconographer eaten too much cheese the night before? It defied explanation, but after I took a photo of it my digital camera went dead and never recovered, despite it being perfectly fine moments earlier. It was a remote church on a hilltop, reputed to have very old and well-preserved frescos, and we had to track down the local keyholder to gain entry.

When we got to the church and unlocked the door, our dog Wallace refused to enter – a sure sign the place had a macabre back story. It certainly felt cold and while some of the Byzantine frescos were indeed splendid, it had a very unwelcome aura, even before we found the two-faced fresco. The keyholder later shed some light on this when he explained that an escape tunnel had been built underneath the church centuries ago – during skirmishes with the Turks – leading to a now-crumbling stone house on the hillside. During the Greek War of Independence in the 19th century a priest had hidden in the tunnel and eventually perished down there. I could well believe it and the fact the church felt haunted.

Some churches look strange or forbidding even before you get inside, or the location is gorgeous but eerie. But nothing we'd seen in Greece could top the eccentric church of Ayia Theodora in Arcadia. It's a suitable region, in the Peloponnese, for an ecclesiastical irregularity as it's known for its rugged mountains and mythological sprites like Pan, the god of forests and shepherds, half-man, half-goat, who played his pipes and repulsed the local nymphs.

In the midst of a thick forest, outside the village of Vasta, stood a tiny stone church with nothing outstanding in its design except for one gigantic, neck-tingling thing: a towering copse of trees sprouting up from its tiled roof. A natural wonder, you might think, but the locals are adamant that this is a miraculous phenomenon and that the church is the physical incarnation of a local martyred saint, Ayia Theodora, after whom it is named. I wrote a version of this story for our website blog while we were living in Greece and it remains the most visited and searched-for blog post I've ever written about this country, and shows no sign of waning.

The day we visited, the sun was blisteringly hot, the temperature nudging 40 degrees, and yet the area around the church, with its spring outlet oozing into an adjacent stream, seemed cool and energising. Although we'd already seen pictures of the church, you can't grasp the eccentricity of the construction until you see it close up. It's a diminutive stone building with what looks like a stiff, over-gelled hairdo consisting of around 17 tall maple and holly trees shooting up to the sky. I don't believe there's anything else like it in the world. You get a sense that something extraordinary happened here a long time ago.

The area definitely had an aura on that hot day, with its thick, surrounding forest, a gentle susurrus of leaves, and the sound of pilgrims shuffling quietly about. It was serene, and not one pilgrim complained about us having Wallace on his lead, taking him around the church or dunking him in the adjacent stream to keep him cool, something that Greeks might normally have a strop over.

The church is of plain construction with a slate roof that seems perfectly at ease with the mini-forest sprouting from it. You ask yourself: how do the trees grow? And will they come crashing down if a wind whips up? We trailed around the outside of the church and were struck by the fact you can't see any evidence of root growth, even with the lower trunks of a couple of trees nudging through the walls below the roof. At the front of the church above the door is the only base of a tree you can really see. It's dark brown, gnarled and apparently very old, and as wide as the door itself. Yet, again, you can't see evidence of a root system.

Inside it's a confined space with a sanctuary behind a simple carved arch, the walls slightly damp with traces of faded frescos, probably painted centuries ago. Even on close inspection you can't find a single trace of a tree trunk or root network anywhere, though you know the roots must be there straining for the spring water below. The impression is that the trees are growing straight up out of the layers of roof tiles, as if floating on air, which of course is theoretically impossible.

Trees were said to have started growing sometime after the church was built in the 10th century, and the ones there today are, presumably, their descendants. It may be a natural, freakish phenomenon, but the locals firmly believe this is a sacred place and that the structure is the miraculous form of Saint Theodora, a martyr saint, who is said to have prayed before her untimely death for her body to be turned into a church, her hair to become a forest of trees above, her blood a stream.

The story of Ayia Theodora's life is more bizarre than the church, even for the often-ghoulish Byzantine era in which it originated. In the 9th century, the pious Theodora wished to join an Arcadian monastery, yet for reasons we'll never understand decided against a women's monastery. She disguised herself as a young man and joined a male establishment instead, changing her name to Theodoros, the male equivalent of her own name, and no-one was any the wiser apparently. And there, at least, began her earthly trials.

While on a mission in the local area to raise funds for her monastery's charitable work, she came across a nun from a nearby establishment, who confessed she was pregnant. This cunning and desperate creature seized on poor 'male' Theodoros and decided to claim he was the father of her child, supposedly in a bid to protect her real lover. Again, for reasons that are blurred with time, Theodoros kept her real gender a secret and decided to take the blame for the pregnancy as a mark of compassion for the nun's plight. Theodoros was eventually tried for this moral lapse and sentenced to death by decapitation.

As the story goes, when the executioner and his cohorts saw Theodoros's body before burial, they realised the monk's gender deception, even if, like us, they couldn't fathom the doolally reasoning behind it. They repented their act and built a church to honour the proper St Theodora, her good deeds and her martyrdom. It was while she was awaiting execution that she uttered her prayer with the wish to be literally turned into a church. So it seems she got what she wished for.

The church may not be on a par with other sacred shrines around the globe, but it can't be far off. It attracts thousands of pilgrims from all over the world, who keep vigil in the shaded forecourt of the church. Some pilgrims have claimed miraculous kinds of healing during their visits, though most of this is undocumented.

On a more prosaic note, the church has also attracted engineering experts over the years from Greek and overseas universities to probe the unaccountable tree sprouting. No-one has been able to explain how the walls have been able to withstand the growth of roots through them for more than 1,000 years without the tiny structure crumbling. A visiting Greek engineer, Eleftherios Beligiannis, once noted that the weight of the trees on the roof would be around nine tons, which is four times greater than what would normally be tolerated by a structure of this size and age. Added to this, during times of high winds and rain there would be an even bigger, more disastrous load on the building.

So miraculous comes fairly close, and certainly Orthodox priests of the past have declared "the will of God overcomes the order of nature". Whether or not you believe such things, the church is worth a visit, as is the whole of Arcadia for its sylvan solitude and fascinating mix of mountains, plains and myths and legends. But even if you like the idea of roof forests, it's one innovation you might not want to try at home.

Only one other church comes close to Ayia Theodora for atmosphere and a strange tree phenomenon. It also proves that if you want to discover a tree with mystical cred, take a dog with you. It was Wallace who discovered an odd-looking specimen in the walled garden of a monastery north of Koroni, in Messinia. Ayioi Theodoroi (no relation to Ayia Theodora but dedicated to several other saints called Theodoros) was a deserted site. It was steeped that afternoon in shadows from a verdant hillside at its edge, with only the sound of a nearby stream to break the rural silence.

We'd planned to inspect the Byzantine church first of all, reputed to have significant old frescos, but Wallace had other ideas, and with the typical questing nature of the Jack Russell terrier he pulled us over to a side garden, to a gnarled-looking tree. Whatever lured him there was probably not what jagged our attention because the closer we got to it the more we could see that on a great swathe of bare trunk was a 'carving' of a large closed hand, with the thumb pointing downwards. I say carved, but it looked too smooth for a human carving. It was roughly two feet by two feet in size and like something fashioned more from wind and rain perhaps, over many decades. Or was it something more mysterious?

We decided on the fanciful name of The Hand of God Tree, given its surroundings, and found it curiously appealing, as Wallace had, even though he hadn't thought to vandalise it, as dogs do. As we'd discovered on many trips to churches and monasteries in Greece, Wallace didn't care for most of them: too cold, too damp, too spooky. When we took him inside, often he whimpered to be let out again. I began to believe that Wallace, like most dogs, had a superior nose for the raw deeds of other centuries, and the traces they left behind. And this monastery, according to the historical notes we'd read, had its fair share of dastardly history.

Built in the 12th century, it had been subjected to various atrocities of the Ottoman Turks in the 16th century, with the mass murder of at least 40 monks in a fire. In more recent times it was the scene of the murder of a lone monk in the 1920s, when the monastery was deserted. He had set up home in the crumbling, abandoned sleeping quarters and became the victim of a vicious attack. The crime was never solved.

The keys to the monastery buildings had been provided by a local priest, Papa Theodoros (a popular name and no relation to any of the others and certainly not a Theodora in the making!). When we returned the keys at his village house, we couldn't wait to show him the photos we'd taken of The Hand of God Tree. We scrolled through them for him, on the back of the camera. He was intrigued, smiling at the moniker we'd given the tree, but when I asked him who or what might have created the hand, he stroked his long beard. I expected him to come up with a good tale, ecclesiastical or otherwise.

"I have no idea what made this shape. It is curious," he said, with the twitch of an amused smile. "I don't think I've ever seen this mark on the tree before. I don't go much into that part of the monastery, I admit." It was typical, in my experience, that rural priests were often a pragmatic bunch, not given over to fanciful notions or revelations, as non-Greeks might expect. They were mostly from poorer farming communities and saw the priesthood as a decent way to earn a living. Many had a very basic education, although that didn't apply to Papa Theodoros exactly. But he had that underwhelmed approach, which I found quite charming.

His wife, however, came to the rescue and seemed to think it was a very old carob tree, yet she too couldn't remember seeing the 'hand' before. The *papas* took the camera for a moment, sat down for a closer look at the photos and seemed introspective.

"Is it something religious, miraculous even?" I suggested, not giving up.

"It's a beautiful idea but the truth is – I don't know," he said with a shrug of apology, yet lingering a while over the images.

Whatever he thought it was, he was keeping it to himself for now. All he would say was that the next time he visited the monastery he would investigate the phenomenon and report back to us.

When we returned to Koroni from our Arcadian visit, I was swimming in a cove not far from Kalamata one day and chatted to an old man paddling nearby, who said he came, co-incidentally, from Vasta. I raved on about the roof trees and asked him what he thought. Something natural or divine? He took a long time to answer and sounded infuriatingly like Papa Theodoros.

"I really don't know, my friend. People in Vasta believe in the story of Ayia Theodora turning into a church. How do we know? You believe it or you don't."

"Which way are *you* leaning though – natural event or divine?" I pressed him. He shrugged his bony shoulders.

"No-one will ever know. Is that not the way we prefer it so we can wonder, believe, talk about it? Why must everything have an explanation?" he said, with a huffy expression. "And if we cannot grasp the miracle, does it mean we don't believe in religion any more?" He started to swim away. "It just IS!" was his parting shot.

So many unusual things in Greece have no explanation at all. It's a land with a surfeit of myths and mysteries you just can't crack. I suspect Wallace had the answer – but he wasn't saying!

(At the time of writing this book, The Hand of God Tree remains a mystery – just like the fantastic roof trees of Ayia Theodora.)

6

The recipe for Greekness

WHAT you eat in Greece, where and with whom, is all you ever need to worry about – up to a point. During the time I've spent in Greece, I've discovered the power of sharing a meal with locals and how unlikely friendships can be forged, even when you're not having the food of your dreams.

In the Mani we were invited several times to villagers' houses on special feast days at Easter and on August 15th, the Assumption of the Virgin Mary. Once we were coaxed into trying the Maniot 'delicacy' of small pickled thrushes, *tsikles*, the capture of which has no delicacy about it. Neither has the sight of them lined up on a plate still bearing their heads. Our fellow diners smiled at our attempts to peel off a few shreds to try, which to the local mind was picky and very 'British'. One bear of a man lost patience and picked up a bird for a demonstration, snapping off the head with his teeth. I can still hear the hollow sound of a skull being crunched. But the fact we'd even tried a morsel of the birds gave us a mild kind of kudos in the eyes of these locals. The equivalent would be eating witchetty grubs (like fat bald caterpillars) in Australia, or 'hundred-year eggs' in the Far East, or drinking kava in Fiji, which I once did. It's a muddy, foul concoction that gets you drunk from the legs up (seriously!), so that after a modest amount, your mind is crystal clear but you're flat out on the floor.

The invitation to a meal, particularly on a saint's day, is part of the ethos of Greek hospitality, *filoxenia* (love of the foreigner/stranger), though I have jokingly called these experiences 'extreme hospitality' at times.

One of the most awkward dining experiences I've had was in Crete in the 1970s while travelling with a university friend. We were renting a rough *spitaki* (small village house) near a beach west of Hania, and the neighbours invited us to Easter Sunday lunch. I had only ever spoken briefly to these people in my rudimentary Greek, learnt a few years earlier while working in Athens. The house was an old stone place, rustic but comfortable, and the outside table on a long veranda was crowded with kids and relatives, all sitting down to feast on roast lamb, lemon potatoes and boiled spring greens – the usual spread after the Lenten fast.

The only problem was that my friend and I were then vegetarians, much rarer in those days and considered a kind of hippy fad. There was no way we were going to break that, even for Greek Easter. And so began a tormenting effort on my part to explain in poor Greek what a vegetarian was and why eating meat was shunned by us. Nothing I said seemed to convince the family that we weren't crazy. "Not eat roast lamb at Easter, *po, po, po*!" the grandmothers tutted, while the children giggled. The wife, Maria, looked mortified that she couldn't please us with a proper lunch, a point of honour for rural Greeks back then.

In a moment of desperation I had the mad idea of telling them we were strict Buddhists, which was why we didn't eat meat, as if that could even seem vaguely logical for two Western visitors in an era when a Buddhist to a rural Greek would have seemed like an alien from outer space. But somehow it worked. I've since discovered that with awkward social situations, the more extreme/bizarre explanations are, the more they're believed. Now when I think of Crete at Easter, I think of that day and Maria serving us just potatoes (mounds of them) and boiled greens and her pitying looks. But we all drank plenty of the family's homemade wine, laughed a lot and the day was quite wonderful.

During trips to Greece of varying lengths I've always marvelled at the sensual partnership between Greeks and food. It's not simply the joy of eating good wholesome food in fabulous locations, especially at a remote beachside taverna, with a roll of waves in the distance and Greek music on an old radio set. The Greek ritual of sharing a meal together is a social and cultural mainstay, as inviolable as taking Holy Communion.

Through good times, and especially bad (and Greece has had an oversupply of those), the Greek meal has been the thread that has united the community, family and strangers. This is particularly so with a meal at a village *yiorti* (celebration), usually the feast day of a particular saint, where tables and chairs are often set under the olive trees. The local priest and village elders will be sitting beside goat farmers, olive harvesters, the rich and the poor, all enjoying lively *parea* (company), good village food and local wine.

In all the years I've been going to Greece I recall there have been few meals with Greeks that didn't reveal the character and philosophy of these lovable but often complex people. On rare occasions the invitations to dine have seemed at odds with the circumstances, or the timing was all wrong, but still they have not disappointed. And once or twice there have been meals I have not wanted to attend at all but which have, curiously, yielded the greatest insight.

Years ago Jim and I were visiting the island of Santorini for a two-week break and a chance to unwind from a difficult year in which I had just lost my mother to cancer. I was seeking sun and solitude and certainly not much company. We had booked a small villa at a luxury hotel complex with a stunning pool and spectacular views over the island's famous volcanic caldera. The first few days were bliss, with hours spent around the pool and quiet meals on the garden terrace. But one day the head waiter, Takis, when he discovered we were journalists and I spoke some Greek, suggested we might like to meet a 'traditional island man' and local character called Artemios, who lived nearby and often trailed through the gardens with his skinny dog, Irma, stopping to chat to Takis at the outside bar. Unusually for me, the idea didn't appeal. I had no urge to do anything on this trip but be lazy. One day, however, Takis introduced us to 'traditional man' by chance and he seemed interesting.

Artemios was 80 but very slim and spry for his age, with a good sense of humour. He kindly invited us for lunch at his *spitaki* the next day. It could do no harm, we reasoned, and then we could return to indolence for the first week at least. Artemios's *spitaki* was not far from the back perimeter fence of the hotel complex but was another world entirely. It overlooked the other side of the island, less dramatic than the soaring cliffs of the caldera on the inside edge of Santorini. Here, in contrast, the hillside sloped gently down to the famous black volcanic beaches.

A stony path led us through his rickety farm compound, with various sheds for goats and chickens, and a donkey was tied to an olive tree. Piles of empty bottles were stacked outside a stone wine press for his own homemade brew. A vegetable patch was tumbling over with fat sweet tomatoes, aubergines and long runners of courgettes as big as marrows. Fig and orange trees and *frangosika* (prickly pear), with their fat spiky leaves like ping-pong bats, completed this idyllic setting. Artemios was dressed in rural style: dusty, baggy jeans held up with a piece of string wound through the tags. He was sunburnt, with pale blue eyes, and wore a frayed straw hat. In some ways he seemed like the male version of the inimitable Foteini we were yet to meet one day in the Mani.

His *spitaki* was small with simple balconies on two sides with a million-pound view of the beaches beyond. A wooden table was set outside for lunch on the cooler side balcony and Irma the dog slept nearby under a rustic bench. An ancient transistor radio was hanging by a piece of wire, playing bluesy Greek tunes. As we were to discover, when the mood took him Artemios would stop what he was doing and slip into a slow Greek dance around the balcony, like an old blue-eyed Zorba.

Lunch was a simple affair: small fried fish with eggplant and Greek salad, with a jug of his own wine. Initially conversation was hard work as I tried to crank up my rusty Greek. But my journalistic curiosity, as always, got the better of me and I persisted with Greek over lunch, smoothed by a few glasses of the honey-flavoured wine. Artemios was patient with my Greek and remarkably good company, and for the next few hours we talked and laughed, listened to the radio, even danced as well, while the dog sloped off to hide under an oleander bush.

This kind of spontaneous hospitality was not unusual in those days in Greece, but even still I wondered why Artemios would want to spend an afternoon with two foreigners, especially when I was the only one really communicating, and

I had to stop regularly to translate much of the conversation for Jim. My only thought was that, with his wife recently having passed away, he was lonely, despite several children living in the nearby village of Imerovigli. However, the fact that we both shared a recent bereavement only served to heighten our rapport. I decided to make the most of this memorable experience because I felt sure we wouldn't go to his house for lunch again. We would treat it as a wonderful 'thing of the moment', in the Greek way. Yet it was as if he'd read my mind when he clinked his wine glass against ours.

"We must do this again quite soon, yes?"

This was tricky. I didn't want to hurt his feelings. I'd already decided we must return his generosity and invite him to the hotel for lunch near the end of our stay. But having to make another definite plan for lunch at his *spitaki* felt awkward in the context of this holiday. And, generally, Greeks don't do plans.

"Oh, we don't want to intrude, and you've been so generous already. Next time we must invite you to lunch."

"Pah, generous! It was a simple meal, that's all. And look, we're not talking about returning a business lunch, my friends. We Greeks are different. Now we've shared a meal together at my house, the three of us, we're friends forever!" he said, with emphasis, slapping Jim warmly on the back before I had time to translate his words.

I was touched by the sentiment. Artemios had espoused in a few sentences the pared-down, easy Greek philosophy of sharing a simple meal and forging a friendship, a bond, 'forever'. There was also a point of honour in it for all of us. It wasn't something you could easily ignore, or talk your way out of, not when he added, "So, you will come another day soon? For another lunch?"

I thought about it a moment, twisting my glass around on the table top. He watched me intently, his pale blue eyes slightly watery in the afternoon glare.

"We'll try," I said vaguely. I was afraid to make promises I would later not want to keep, or to bind Jim to long lunches with endless Greek chatter when there were places on the island I knew he wanted to see before we left. Artemios watched me with increasing Greek impatience.

I didn't want to be pressed over this, but when someone offers you the hand of friendship, however it's been motivated, it's hard to refuse, especially in Greece with its warm heart and 'traditional' characters, who in 2002 were beginning to be harder to find. His words seemed to cast some kind of spell over my recent bereavement, my reclusiveness. To hell with it, I thought, let's do another lunch.

We ended up going to his house a few more times. One time we also dined with an old friend of his from Athens, a jovial guy who liked a good wind-up, a fair slug of ouzo and the odd *zeibekiko* dance thrown in, with the radio turned up to the max. By the end of the afternoon, he had us all dancing around the balcony, the music and laughter wafting up the hill towards the edge of the villa complex, which was quiet and shuttered in the siesta hours.

Takis the waiter chortled when he saw us traipsing back, slightly tipsy from lunch. He said with a wink, "You spend big money to stay at this beautiful hotel and you would rather be with our *horiates* (villagers), eh?" We laughed. It was his fault after all.

We saw a lot of Artemios in the following week and treated him to dinners in nearby Imerovigli. We met some of his family and other friends. I found that meeting Artemios and making that warm connection helped me through a dark time in my life and left me few opportunities to brood over it. And I liked to think that maybe the friendship had helped Artemios in his bereavement as well. In its way, it had been a fateful event for both of us.

When we returned to Scotland, that feeling hovered over me as normal life resumed. One day I opened a tin of

Santorini tomatoes that Artemios had insisted we take in our hand luggage when we left, along with a bag of pungent fresh capers, the aroma of which we seemed to drag behind us like a nippy slipstream. I opened the tin of tomatoes and on the top found a white feather, obviously from a roosting bird in a rural canning factory. Jim and I laughed over this find, as if it had been something Artemios had devised to make us think of Santorini. And we did.

I wrote to him regularly in the months ahead and also started Greek language evening classes once a week at Edinburgh University because the holiday had highlighted my poor Greek and laziness about improving it years after I'd first started to learn it. The following year we returned to Santorini for another two weeks and continued our lunching routine with Artemios and became even better friends.

While we were unable to return to Santorini, for many different reasons, in the years that followed, I kept up a correspondence with him for a long time and often phoned him. However, one day a letter arrived from his granddaughter to say that despite his seemingly robust health, Artemios had passed away after a short illness. I was sad when I heard the news, as if I had lost a family member and I felt guilty too that we hadn't seen him before he died. But I have never forgotten him.

To share a simple meal with Greeks, or anyone for that matter, and then be friends forever on the strength of it is wonderful. In this life, it doesn't get much better than that.

7

Hearts in exile

ON the second leg of our Greek odyssey in 2014, we stayed for a year in Koroni, at the tip of the Messinian peninsula. While the location brought new friends and connections among the Greek community, it also put other groups into the frame. It was here that we had an experience that conveyed the tight, sometimes fateful connections between Greek North Americans and their spiritual homeland. What I discovered also opened up a poignant seam of reflection about my own life that I hadn't examined in years, as a Scot having migrated with my family to Australia at an early age.

In Koroni, in the spring, we started visiting a small secluded beach on the side of town facing the Ionian Sea. At the back of sandy Zaga beach is a set of stone steps leading to the gate of a lovely old property, a white house in a shady garden. Its best feature was the huge round table made of stone on a thick plinth, with stone seating around one side, as if designed for a family of forest giants. The place gave the sense of Greek ownership and I could imagine a big garrulous group sitting there on summer afternoons sharing a meal and dashing down to the sea now and then for a cooling dip. I often imagined who the owners might be and would have laid bets on Athenians who only came mainly for the August holidays. But in a quirk of fate I was to find out sooner than I expected.

After my first book *Things Can Only Get Feta* was published in North America, in May 2014, I had a few emails to our website from readers, and one in particular from a friendly Canadian called Alexia, who had a special interest in the book as her family originally came from Kalamata and the Mani. We exchanged emails and she told me she had spent a few summers in the southern Peloponnese, visiting relatives and friends.

When I mentioned living in Koroni, she emailed me a photo of her father on a beach. I recognised it straight away – Zaga, the beach with the stone steps. I quizzed her about the house and she told me it was owned by a Canadian friend of her father's, not an Athenian. He had often visited and so had she, a couple of times in past years. There had been long summer lunches too, just as I'd imagined.

It was a strange coincidence, but not where Greece is concerned. The longer I stay connected with Greece, the more I recognise the tight webbing between this country and the Greek diaspora (the dispersed populations, and fittingly a Greek word) in Canada and America, and Australia too. These were the families who had to leave, often for economic reasons, but most often for political freedom after the German occupation in World War Two, the ensuing disastrous Greek civil war, and the military dictatorship of the 1960s and 70s. The diaspora were people who never forgot their country or their faith and whose family connections between the two places continue to spread and flourish.

From the connections I've made with American Greeks in particular, I'm always impressed by their passion for

Greece and how most of them still talk about the country as if they or their families had never left it, sharing pictures on social media, reminiscences and anecdotes. Many talk longingly of their next holidays there in the summer, counting off the days, even though most have successful, happy lives in America. But to these people Greece is still their *patrida*, their homeland, even those born and bred in America. Although her family left Greece when they were young, decades ago, Alexia said her feelings about Greece were surprisingly strong. "It's crazy to feel so connected to a place that my brother, sister and I have only really visited a handful of times."

The feelings of the diaspora for their homeland rings true for me as well because it reflects that of the Scottish diaspora and mass migration from Scotland over the past three centuries. After historic skirmishes with the English, the infamous Highland Clearances were put into effect in the 18th and 19th centuries, when around 250,000 poor tenant farmers of the highlands and islands like Skye, and Harris and Lewis, were violently evicted from their land and their croft houses and their villages were burnt to the ground. Most were forced on to ships sailing to places like Nova Scotia and the Quebec region in east Canada, never to return. The Clearances have their roots in the British establishment's desire to break the Scottish clan system, and the land secured during this time was given over to more lucrative sheep farming.

In more recent years, after the poverty of the post-war era, the Scots left of their own accord mostly, seeking an easier lifestyle and economic opportunities, lured mainly in the 1960s and 70s by the Australian government's 'assisted migration scheme' to Australia, the famous £10 boat ticket. My family left Perth, Scotland, for Sydney on the SS Orontes on this scheme. It was a no-frills, six-week voyage, with compulsory schooling and segregated accommodation, with families split into male- and female-only cabins. For kids it felt like a glorious holiday, with nothing to do but swim in the pool and eat three filling meals a day, but there were hardships on the way: lack of space and privacy, and the searing heat at the equator. Even then, it had the unexpected bonus of being able to sleep on the decks (the sexes segregated). I still have an image in my mind of women, with just sheets and pillows, lying out in rows with their children, talking well into the night, singing sometimes, with infectious camaraderie and hopes for a new life ahead.

In these same decades Greeks also left their homeland in droves, jaded by war and political upheaval, craving opportunity in the 'new world'. Both groups, wherever they settled, punched above their weight in terms of the contributions they made to their new countries with hard work, thriving businesses and entrepreneurial spirit. During my life I've shared the cultures of both these groups of migrants, starting at a young age in Australia as a migrant, and ironically my first real school friend was Anna, a first-generation Greek migrant. I quickly became part of her extended family and had a vibrant baptism into her life and culture. It was a fortuitous circumstance that set my path towards Greece forever more.

There are startling similarities in the Scottish and Greek migrant experience, but the latter probably had the edge in that the larger, close-knit families were able to help each other to establish networks, setting up businesses, schools and churches. This is true, especially in cities in North America like Chicago, with its famous Greektown, a vibrant area created in the 1840s by Greeks to provide their own cuisine and ethnic lifestyle and which morphed into a successful neighbourhood that boomed between the 1970s and 90s. Today Chicago has the third largest Greek settlement in the US.

The Greeks and Scots have had much in common and a great optimism for change wherever they settled. Yet they often shared something deeper as well: times of heartbreaking challenge and simmering resentment for the circumstances of their leaving, or in the case of highland Scots, their violent expulsion. Inevitably there was searing nostalgia for the homeland.

I am always moved by the way in which these two groups have equally mined their heartbreak and loss in cultural outpourings, particularly in their beautiful and haunting songs. No-one can hear a Scottish highland folk song and not feel heartsore by the migrant experience, especially that of the Gaelic people of the highlands and islands, who have produced perhaps the richest heritage of songs of exile in the world. The popular Gaelic song *Chi Mi Na Morbheanna* (The Mist Covered Mountains, written by John Cameron) being a classic example, an instrumental version of which was featured on the soundtrack of the iconic film *Local Hero*, set in north-east Scotland. The words to this song are simple but flag up the yearning to go back home.

Similarly, in the early 19th century, Gaelic fishermen on the St Lawrence River, in the Quebec region of Canada, sang a touching lament of exile that has become legendary among the Scottish diaspora of North America and beyond.

"*From the lone shieling of the misty island*
Mountains divide us, and the waste of seas
Yet still the blood is strong, the heart is Highland
And we in dreams behold the Hebrides"

The sentiment of the poem found expression in the album *The Blood Is Strong* (Survival Records) by the Gaelic folk group Capercaillie, with acclaimed singer Karen Matheson, and was the title of a 1980s Channel 4 TV documentary about Gaelic history and emigration.

The Greeks too have produced a rich seam of traditional songs that tap into the same sense of nostalgia and longing for the Greece they left behind, like the popular song from the northern region of Epirus, *Ksenitemeno Mou Pouli* (My loved one who has gone abroad). Nostalgia is a Greek word and Greeks have become its long-term exponents. The Greek word *ksenitia* means 'abroad' or 'foreign lands', but it means so much more to Greek people. According to Margarita Nikolopoulou, an Athenian teacher and poet, "The word *ksenitia* is a loaded word for Greeks and bears all the burden of being a migrant."

She says the expression *O kaimos tis ksenitias* (the torment of foreign lands) speaks for the migrant, as well as those loved ones left behind who miss their family. "For the migrant, this expression is not just about nostalgia for home, it encapsulates all the suffering, obstacles and loneliness of being abroad. It's a highly charged expression."

In my experience of migration, while life may become easier, the nostalgia and '*kaimos*' never fades – and sometimes it goes the other way. Despite decades living in Australia, my family always called Scotland 'home'. "We're going home next year for a holiday," they would say, as if the lives they had so painstakingly etched out for themselves in Australia were nothing but a temporary fix. Which they weren't. One dear aunt, still living in Sydney and now in her nineties, used to go back to Scotland with her husband every other year as long as I can remember, until she was too old and frail to make the trip.

Scots, like Greeks, are everywhere in the world, in every far-flung corner. Two very different diaspora but both do exile very well, bettered only perhaps by long-suffering Jewish emigres of past centuries. But while the Scots can keep the emotional fire of nostalgia burning, with a liberal dash of sentimentality thrown like oil to the flames, they are not always good at keeping the cultural rituals of Scotland alive with the same vitality and commitment as the Greeks, not in Australia anyway.

In the past, we tended to float off to our individual lives and endeavours and in a few generations Scottish cultural heritage for many was often diluted, if not the abiding love for Scotland. Perhaps it's inevitable when the Scots (apart from the Gaelic families of the western isles in previous centuries) haven't had to adopt a new language or a radically different culture, unlike the Greeks, who have forged close networks, especially in North America.

When I hear the stories of Chicago's still-thriving Greektown, I can't imagine this being replicated in places like Australia, though when I was young there were some western suburbs of Sydney where a number of Scots settled and where there were highland events each year with pipe bands and competitions. But there was never the equivalent of a Scotstown.

However, my family *did* keep faith with Scottish celebrations, food and music. I well remember the raucous Hogmanay parties each year in our suburban Sydney backyard, the record player cranked up to the max with old Scottish favourites: the nostalgic and the jubilant, the frenzied reels, the sky-cracking swirl of the bagpipes that would send our family dog skittering down the backyard to hide in the henhouse with the chickens. And the party would often go on like this until dawn. Not that any neighbours ever complained. They probably weren't game enough!

For years I've followed my North American friends' posts on social media and have admired the way they keep the spirit of Greece prominent in their lives, building Greek Orthodox churches to rival many in Greece and sending their kids to Greek language school, supporting the many Greek rituals. Greekness is alive and well in North America, and the Antipodes as well, where Melbourne is said to have the largest population of Greeks outside of Athens.

These two groups also have another similar tendency. When the children of migrants reach adulthood, they generally yearn to go back for a sabbatical to search out their roots. I went back to Scotland when I'd barely left high school, which was a transformative experience, even if it raised more questions for me than answers because once you straddle two countries you can be left with what one Australian writer, now living in Greece, calls "the divided heart". For a few voyagers, however, the homeland holiday won't be enough and eventually they will yearn to pack up and go back for good.

My mother in the early years in Australia often spoke longingly about returning home, crying for the things she'd left behind, comically so at times – the yearning for real Scottish bacon on a bap (morning roll). But at that point it wasn't possible for us to return 'home' and as the years wore on, the edges of her despair were quietly bevelled away.

However, some do make it in the end. I vividly recall meeting a Canadian Greek couple in Kalamata, who had gone to Greece to reconnect with their homeland with only one problem – they opened a small restaurant in the city just as the economic crisis was beginning to bite in 2010. They built up a thriving business yet, a few years later, they were struggling and had to return to Canada, broken-hearted, because mentally they had already reconnected with Greece and having to return to Canada was ironically repeating the angst of emigration their own parents had once endured.

The migrant experience is a complex web of emotions, fears and frustrations that most people will absorb in the end to the benefit of themselves and the host country, but I have met some Scots and Greeks in various parts of the world whose hearts in exile have never healed. For some migrants it's more than just harking after the old ways of life, for 'your ain folk', it's a visceral longing for the unique beauty of the actual places left behind.

You understand this better when you go back yourself. I had only distant memories of Perth, a small city with an historic layout, sheltered by surrounding hills, before I left as a child, but in the flesh, it was unimaginably beautiful. Standing one day on the banks of the wide River Tay, with its elegant stone bridge and peaty salmon-filled water roiling below, I wondered rather youthfully why anyone would want to leave such a place. How was my family able to turn away and sail to the other side of the world, away from all this? Cold weather notwithstanding, it must have been with great difficulty, when I considered my mother's daily laments.

Migration must have been even harder at times in Greece, a country of endless sunshine, pristine blue sea and glorious islands of famed, minimalistic beauty that draw tourists like magnets. I've seen how easy it is for most Greeks in Australia to reconstruct their sunny, laid-back Greek way of life – often comically so, with the odd Doric column at the front door – and I've admired them for it. Yet I also know that no matter how much they dance or sing about them, the places Greek migrants remember, with their well-honed, traditional ways of life, are probably gone forever.

The Mani, where we lived for three years in Greece, is starkly beautiful: remote, rural, uncompromising, in the shadow of the Taygetos mountains. But in the past the climate and the aridity of the soil and its far-flung location sired many thousands of economic migrants, emptying hillside villages that have never really recovered.

One summer, while travelling around some of these villages, we came upon one that was hosting a big Greek wedding for a family from Chicago that would, by tradition, go on for days. The village was alive with noise, music, life, and the small permanent population was vastly outnumbered. The locals told us it made a change from the normal quiet routine of life, but some of the older residents confessed the wedding had spiked a painful nostalgia for happier days when this was a real village, filled with people, filled with life, something they'd never experience again – unless there was another Chicago family's wedding.

I remember a story from an American man who went back to the Mani to find his roots. Although the location was beautiful, he found his ancestral home in ruins, the village near-deserted, like the one mentioned above, with few permanent residents. He lamented that it was hard to find any villager who could actually remember who his family had been. With first- and second-generation descendants of migrants, I sense the loss they must feel for a culture many of them don't fully understand and a language many don't speak. There's also a sense of anger sometimes for the circumstances that forced their families out in the first place and robbed them of a heritage that now may seem like a mirage that fades the closer they get to it. That was a sentiment I felt at times in my own upbringing in Australia.

When Jim and I decided to return permanently to Scotland in 2000, I took my widowed mother as well, which I touched on briefly in *Things Can Only Get Feta*. She was dubious at first about returning, despite all the tears she'd shed early on for this very thing. I suspect she was also frightened that as a permanent home Scotland wouldn't stack up now in comparison with the breezy optimism of Australia. In the end, that wasn't the case for either of us. This was a different Scotland to the post-war country we'd left. A year after devolution, this was a nation with optimism of its own.

One of the outcomes of going back to Scotland to live wasn't just discovering the searing beauty and wildness of the land my family had given up. I finally understood the why and the how of leaving, the imperatives that drove migration: punishing winters, the poverty of the era, stretching for many years after the Second World War, and the lack of opportunity, more so when I revisited childhood haunts with my mother as guide and heard her stories of early hardship. For both of us, returning to Scotland in 2000 had finally been a revelation, with the knowledge that my parents had made an inspired decision after all, in the times they had lived through. Scotland was now on a better trajectory as well. The awkward space in the circle had been filled at last.

As for my Canadian friend Alexia, she wrote to me saying she would be going back to Koroni again in the near future with her family and we should meet up perhaps. I envisaged a lunch around the stone table in the shady garden. I could already see her family crammed around it, full of happy chatter, sharing a typical Greek meal, with the sea just a few stone steps away.

It reminds me that one final thread unites the Scottish and Greek diasporas. Even if our heritage isn't our full entitlement any more, or completely within our grasp, we can still own the spirit of it. And no-one can ever take that away from us.

8

Driving yourself mad in Greece

WHEN we dreamt up our Greek odyssey for 2010, we decided to drive the whole way in our old Ford Fiesta because we wanted to take as much luggage as we could, and we had Wallace our crazy terrier with us. Leaving him with someone in Scotland, or even going by plane to Greece and putting him in a dog-friendly cargo hold, was never an option. I had heard alarming stories of dogs being manhandled on planes. And the idea of poor Wallace being locked up in the cargo hold was frightening. What mayhem might he dream up alone in the belly of an aircraft?

We planned to do the overland trip in five days: an unhurried jaunt through France, Switzerland and Italy, then an overnight ferry trip from Ancona to Patras in western Greece. The journey was easier and more exciting than we'd imagined, even the dog-friendly cabin on the ferry was a great success, for Wallace mostly.

The car was packed to the gunnels, with an engine not as powerful as we might have liked. As we planned to be away for a year, or hopefully longer, we aimed to sell the Ford after the first six months and buy a Greek car because at that point the only other option was to keep driving the UK car illegally, and risk a massive fine, or re-registering it in Greece. Only mad foreigners with deep pockets and a high tolerance for bureaucracy ever attempted this method. We couldn't trade in the Ford as it was right-hand drive and only fit to be plundered for parts by that time. We did sell it to a Greek family in our first village of Megali Mantineia for a token amount. Some of the men in the family had a taste for stripping or reconditioning old bangers, which were parked in the road outside their house.

Buying a Greek car was no easy matter, however, and meant visiting a slew of car yards in Kalamata, listening to endless sales patter, with no idea if the cars we saw were just buffed-up heaps of junk or worth the inflated price that the salesman scrawled, in nearly every case, on a dusty windscreen. After a whole day of haggling, we decided it would have been easier buying a gypsy caravan pulled by an ancient mule with a sway back.

Tired and fed-up by the end of the day, our ears near to bleeding from the endless sales hyperbole, we sloped into the last car yard on the block. The assistant was young, genial and keen to let us try out a small Fiat Panda. So off we roared, with the guy in the passenger seat and Jim driving, onto a frantically busy six-lane road connecting Kalamata to the airport, where driving stunts were the order of the day. But the sales guy had one of his own when we reached a massive intersection. As the traffic lights changed to red, he ordered Jim to bust the lights and do a screaming U-turn to get back to the car yard. I saw Jim's eyes in the rear-view mirror –

they were out on stalks – but we got back safely and ended up buying the Fiat, which turned out to be a great car.

As we planned to share the driving in Greece, I now had to master a left-hand vehicle, which I hadn't done much of before, well not for more than 10 minutes anyway, up a dirt track once in Spain. I could handle the British car on Greek roads but couldn't get the hang of the left-hand vehicle with a right-hand gear stick, not helped by poor rural roads, maverick drivers and ambiguous road signs. I had many trial runs along a quiet sea road in the Mani, churning up dirt verges and skirting along the edges of olive groves. I got the hang of it in the end but was never able to thoroughly relax on Greek roads, even though I've always loved driving and have driven on a few different continents.

When we lived for a year in the Messinian peninsula from 2014, it took well over an hour to get from Koroni to Kalamata city (50km), a trip we had to make at least once a week. Jim did most of the driving to Kalamata, but during our first autumn there he had to return to Britain for family reasons and I stayed alone at our house with Wallace. I had to make several trips to Kalamata, however, including one to take Wallace to the vet. Each time I was full of dread.

The road to the city is picturesque but long and narrow, twisty in parts and used by tractors, pick-up trucks and buses. It has poor edges in places, where the road sheers off on to deep drops to nearby fields, with no guard rails. That's before you factor in maverick Greek drivers and long stretches of road with poor visibility, where some daredevil always tries to overtake.

To psych myself up for these trips to Kalamata I decided the only strategy was to treat driving in Greece as a metaphor for life itself. Aim big, I say! And it was this: only focus on the scary, I'm-about-to-die moments when they arise. Take it all one crumbling pothole, one dangerous overtake at a time, minute by minute. Don't think about the whole, long journey, or even the destination, or you'll never arrive – sane!

On the day I took Wallace to see Angelos, our charming vet, I'd forgotten that Petalidi, one of the villages on the way, was having its weekly *laiki* market, which always meant the narrow roads were log-jammed at intersections with tractors, food trucks, buses, gypsy hawkers in pick-up trucks crammed with fruit and veg, with watermelons occasionally bouncing off the back and splattering all over the road.

Of course, this particular route to Kalamata wasn't *always* paved with hellish outcomes. There were calm days too, and the road stretches beside the coastline. If you can ever relax for a moment, the views are gorgeous, looking across the Messinian gulf towards the Mani and the Taygetos mountains, with Kalamata city spread along the head of the gulf. There are moments during this scenic part of the journey when you remember exactly why you wanted to live in Greece. But you can never take your eyes off the road for long. Around every corner is the outrageously unexpected and the close shave, of which we've had many in our time in Greece, including some near head-on collisions.

Driving to Kalamata that morning I saw drivers overtaking on blind bends and coming straight for me (very normal); pick-up trucks loaded with goats (normal, though sometimes it's donkeys – I swear!); one driver hogging a busy stretch of road while a police car desperately needed to overtake and the driver wouldn't budge (Greek rebel, very normal). I also saw a motorbike rider with no helmet (hugely normal) weaving about and awkwardly carrying a large wrapped package under one arm; a couple on another motorbike with two children sandwiched on the seat between them (no helmets) and at least one farmer walking along the road trailing four skittery goats on ropes (less common).

There are animal hazards aplenty on Greek roads, including runaway chickens, and in a hillside village once I had to dodge a horse cantering down the road with no rider or escort. For British drivers, the roads can be terrifying. We knew expats who refused to drive at all, or would only ever motor around their own village. I sympathise with their anxieties, especially in the Mani, where the roads through the Taygetos mountains are full of hairpin bends and sheer drops.

While driving in Greece the bolshy, reckless side of the Greek character always mystified me. I think Greeks are wonderful, generous, unique, and I love them, but why do they go bonkers on the road, breaking every rule in the book, playing with the equivalent of a loaded gun? Ordinarily, I love the Greeks' non-conformist attitude. I love the way they can think for themselves, be bold, and not rely on the nannying attitude we suffer in Britain, but behind the wheel of a car this attitude goes psycho.

Sometimes it's comical, too, like the guy I once saw in Kalamata driving with one knee up around the steering wheel while he rolled himself a cigarette with both hands. I also saw a motorbike rider with a big trombone wedged in his lap, and another biker on a busy city street clutching a tray of takeaway coffees.

Parking is also crazy: cars parked at the head of one-way streets so no-one else can get in or out, or parked across corners or on pavements. What Greeks do while trying to park can sometimes be hilarious. In Kalamata I watched a crazy piece of 'street theatre' when a small two-door car pulled up very close to the pavement on a busy city street. The middle-aged driver opened his door and bashed it against a telegraph pole. His wife, squeezed into the back seat, slapped him vigorously around the head and let out a tirade of oaths about his poor parking skills. Instead of just reversing or moving forward, where he could get the door fully opened, the rotund driver then did something mental – perhaps the result of too many slaps about his cranium. He tried to squeeze himself out of the small gap between car and pole. It was like a hard-boiled egg going through a keyhole, but the gambit failed and he slumped over the steering wheel, breathless. His wife slapped him hard around the head again and bawled a new volley of insults. It drew a crowd of onlookers, most guffawing at the pantomime, and one old guy calling him the Greek equivalent of a dickhead! This was the final straw for the driver. So he wised up and moved the car a few feet forward, clear of the pole. I was mesmerised, wondering why the driver had made life so hard for himself, unless he just liked a bit of rough from his missus now and then. Sometimes you laugh at all this eccentric behaviour. But other times you live in fear.

I have very little good advice to offer the nervous novice driver in Greece apart from this: give way to *everything*, always, even when you have the divine right of way. Let it go, even if it's a slow centenarian riding a bowlegged mule. And get a good insurance broker because if, God forbid, you do have an accident, sorting it out in Greece can be complicated, even if you've got the language skills and can recite the Iliad in Greek – backwards.

While we were in southern Greece during the crisis, it was particularly dodgy because of the number of old heaps on the roads: cars without bumpers, sides bashed in, all kind of bits missing, ancient models belonging in car museums, like something out of Cuba with worry beads. More scarily, cars with bald tyres and dodgy brakes. Many Greeks in the crisis simply didn't have the money to maintain and insure a car, or get MOT and tax for it. Many (sensible) people would hand back their number plates to the tax department and mothball the car until dosh was more forthcoming.

Greeks not only show a spark of maverick ingenuity while driving, but often I had to smile at their ability to wriggle out of trouble on the roads with great panache. One day in Kalamata we saw three young men in a car pulling up illegally onto the start of a pedestrian precinct in the old market sector of the city, next to a busy main road. The three jumped out for a visit to a nearby shop, unfazed by their parking audacity and the arm-waving and moaning of passers-by having to walk around the car. We drank a coffee at a nearby café mainly just to watch the aftermath of the parking. Sure enough, a police car swung by, saw the vehicle, wrote out a ticket and left. When the trio returned and snatched the ticket from under the windscreen wiper they had a big Mediterranean strop, to the amusement of onlookers, us included.

One of the trio must have had a brainwave and lifted the bonnet of the car, pulling out what looked like a spark plug cable. Then he got on his mobile and had a loud chat with what we guessed was a breakdown service, asking for help to start the car. This was obviously a ruse to dodge the parking fine by later writing to the traffic cops to explain the car had broken down and had to be pushed onto the pedestrian area, safely out of the way. But first they had to wait for the breakdown service. I'd love to have known the outcome to this charade, but we had to leave. I don't think it could have been successful, and I'm sure the trio didn't expect it to be. They were like lots of people you meet, especially in southern Greece, who like to put two fingers up to the establishment and break rules – just for the hell of it really, a sentiment we can all sympathise with at times.

Driving into Kalamata that autumn day with Wallace was only the first challenge I faced. The appointment at the vet's was the other. Wallace was never a calm patient. Like most terriers, he didn't like being handled much. I'd asked Angelos to clip his nails because they were too long and needed an expert cutter, with me holding the dog still. As Angelos set about the nail cutting, Wallace wriggled around like an angry ferret in a sack. He was wearing a muzzle but was still snapping and growling.

"Negative, Wallace! Negative!" said Angelos firmly. It was his favourite reprimand, which always made me smile. Wallace was cool for a moment and then started up again, and I could see Angelos's forehead beading with sweat. During a gigantic wriggling episode, the vet accidentally nipped the quick of a nail on a back paw and it started to bleed copiously. No great problem, except that in the consultation room later I had to hold Wallace, still in his muzzle, in my lap, on his back, with his legs up in the air, a wad of tissues squeezed to his paw to stop it dripping blood on the floor. Luckily there was a gap in appointments, but as Angelos was a convivial guy, he had at least two male 'clients' dropping in one after the other to chat about various things, mostly the economic crisis. They sat in the chair next to mine in front of the vet's vast wooden desk. Wallace was mostly fine with all that, but the visitors found it amusing so see the dog on his back, his manhood hanging out, growling softly now and then at imagined intrusions on his precious terrier body, or alarmed by the rattle of small coffee cups on saucers when refreshments were ordered from a nearby café, which is quite normal in many Greek professional situations.

I felt sweaty and hot myself once we'd left and I needed to retreat to a salubrious pavement café on the main Aristomenous Street, where I ordered a chicken sandwich, half of which I passed to Wallace under the table because chicken was the only soother he never refused. Thus fortified, we made our way home, another gauntlet to run. However, it was quieter on the roads in the siesta hours. Not sensible, but less frenetic, and I saw the man from earlier, walking along the edge of the road, leading his goats. I imagined he was on the way home now for an afternoon snooze. Happily, we had all survived another steamy day of mayhem – and that was mostly Angelos the vet!

9

Happy as old Hellas

"CRISIS? What crisis?" was the refrain we regularly heard from the more cynical British expats during our first months in Greece. "Nothing's changed. Everyone's still out and about in the tavernas and cafés just like before," they chirped.

While it was true that the economic crisis wasn't affecting British expats at all, living on UK pensions or accessing their holiday homes for part of the year, it wasn't the same for Greeks. In the first year of the crisis, everyday life gave the impression of normality but you could sense the anxiety bubbling beneath the surface. Through a combination of over-borrowing and fiscal mismanagement, Greece had debts of around 300 billion euros in 2009. The EU had offered a bailout package of 110 billion euros, in return for which a raft of stringent austerity measures was implemented that would be rolled out over the next few years, with wage and pension cuts. Unemployment rates soared.

Having lived in Greece decades earlier, long before anyone had to fester over a fiscal spreadsheet, I sensed very strongly in 2010 that we were in a strange watershed moment. While the country was still suffering the threat of the crisis more than the devastating effects, it felt as if we were also culturally on a tipping point between the old Greece, with its gloriously chaotic remnants of the Levantine narrative of past centuries, and a 'new' kind of Greece. To me, it felt like a heightened moment before Greece was lorded over by the EU and became a place of rules, measures, spreadsheets, and global condemnation for supposed work-shy behaviour and alleged corruption.

In that strange watershed moment, I felt it possible to hold on to and savour the spirit of that unstructured past I was more familiar with – just for a little longer. Most foreigners of a certain age still yearn for the old Greece, as I do, even if it was also underscored by political upheaval carried over by the two world wars and the military junta of the 1960s and 70s. Yet it was still the seductive Greece that lured foreign travellers and creative souls like Leonard Cohen and Australian writers George Johnston and Charmian Clift to islands like Hydra in the 1960s.

It was the 1970s when I first went to Greece, not long after leaving school, and it had the same appeal. When I arrived in Athens and stepped off the overland bus from London, I loved the aura of the place. It was something I wrote about in my second travel memoir, *Homer's Where The Heart Is*: "It was nothing I could easily define, but more a fusion of disparate things, all maddeningly exotic to my young mind: the incomprehensible street signs, the old people dressed in black, the coffee shops, the bakeries wafting aromas of freshly baked bread and the famous cheese pies, and all the other smells, even the bad ones – fetid drains and a city still staggering after a long summer heatwave. It all blended into a heady Levantine cocktail."

The Greece of past decades seemed to have the ability to absorb conflict (and there has been much of that – political and otherwise) and chaos as if it were part of the fabric of its life. The conflict was flagged up with a reverence for individuality and a dislike of rules, lawmakers and civic busybodies. Greece had a breezy, shoulder-shrugging mentality. There's a down side to this, of course, that naturally led to the inability of Greeks to attend to those infamous spreadsheets which escalated the later economic crisis. Yet we all secretly covet the old Hellenic spirit and the freedom it brings.

I still feel real nostalgia for it, not only from my time in Athens but also from my travels through the islands and the rural mainland – nostalgia for a way of life that was simpler, if rougher; where donkeys were more common than cars in rural backwaters; when you bought most of your food at local markets; when yoghurt only came in brown ceramic bowls and the only kind of instant coffee was Nescafe; and where the drachma still reigned and joining the EU seemed like a futuristic fantasy.

Athens was where my love affair with Greece began. In the weeks after I arrived, checking into a cheap city hotel, I roamed the capital constantly, fired up by my school studies in Ancient Greek history. I returned frequently to the Acropolis, and the nearby Agora, a leafy sanctuary in the city. It was once the civic centre of ancient Athens, a place where writers and philosophers such as Plato and Socrates famously strolled, sharing the odd syllogism and some academic craic.

For me, the old neighbourhoods of the city had great appeal, such as the Plaka, built below one side of the

Acropolis; Thissio, which encompassed the Agora and the Temple of Hephaestus; and nearby Monastiraki, a vibrant, colourful quarter with narrow streets, shops and markets, where tradesmen produced traditional folky items: bouzoukis, shoes, rugs, bags, and sought-after metalwork in small back-street foundries. Having spent most of my youth in Australia, a country where nothing was older than the late 18th century, Athens was intoxicating, oozing charm and history, where a simple walk downtown brought you a spectacular offering of archaeology, museums and churches.

One of my favourite places was the ancient burial ground of Kerameikos (derived from the word for pottery, as the cemetery was in the pottery-making quarter of the city). This burial ground has been used since the Bronze Age, but was properly laid out in the 5th century BC by Themistocles, encompassing the city walls and gates, some of which are still visible. The most illustrious citizens of the city were buried here, their graves decorated with sculptures or carved grave markers (*stelae*) and they offer a unique glimpse into Athenian life. One mass grave with over 150 skeletons was discovered in 1994 during excavations for the city's underground Metro railway and is said to be evidence of a plague that swept Athens in 430BC.

Many of the surviving headstones in Kerameikos had elaborate epitaphs, like this curious one I found mentioned in an antiquarian Greek book on the subject:

"The dead are of two kinds, those who return like vrikolakes (vampires) to their beloved places and others who dance lightly in the sky. I am one of those, held in a chain of dancers, led by a god."

After a few weeks in Athens, I liked the place so much I decided to stay and find a job, which I did through the advertising pages of the famous English language paper of its day, *The Athens News*. It was a ritual for expats of all nationalities in those pre-internet days to gather in cafés around Syntagma Square and scour the paper for international news and local gossip. If we were flush with cash, we might have gone nearby to the iconic Zonars café on Panepistimio Street. Opened in 1938 in the style of the literary cafés of Paris, Zonars was classy with heavy décor, huge gilt mirrors, mood lighting and some of the best cakes in the city.

My live-in job entailed working for a married couple in Halandri, north of the city. The husband was Greek, his wife was English and they had a young son, whom I was to look after for part of the day, as well as tutoring him in English. It was a flexible arrangement that allowed me plenty of free time to explore Athens, but also to teach English privately some evenings to supplement my income. There were no requirements for private teaching in those days: no references needed, just a willingness to impart English to middle-class families mostly, keen to learn the language as a means of getting ahead. Now nearly everyone in urban Greece with a reasonable education speaks it. Back then it was rarer.

Those early endeavours in Athens had been so easy to arrange, with great flexibility and little fuss, yet the only negative factor in this youthful new life was a big one, as Greece was living through another tormenting time in its history. In 1967 the country had come under the boot of an infamous military dictatorship that seized power in a coup engineered by army officers, led by Colonel George Papadopoulos. It was brutal and swift, aimed at quelling the alleged leftist influence in the Greek judiciary, press and government departments, and was in its way a continuation of the repressed hatred between the left and the right that had exploded into civil war in the late 1940s.

During the junta years until 1974, martial law was in place and civil liberties were suppressed. Anyone who seemed hostile to the status quo was harassed, arrested and often sent to one of the infamous island prisons. The list of what was outlawed by the colonels was as long as it was illogical at times: the works of 200 Greek and foreign authors were banned, including Shakespeare, Euripides, Artistophanes, and modern writers such as Arthur Miller and Jean-Paul Sartre. Some music, including the works of iconic left-wing composer Mikis Theodorakis, was also banned. In fact, anything thought to have a bad influence on youth or was against Greek Orthodox beliefs was outlawed, including mini-skirts and long hair.

As a young woman who'd had a carefree, sunny life in Australia, the only volatile things we experienced Down Under were Christmas tree lights regularly exploding in 100-degree heat, or garden invasions of deadly funnel web spiders.

When I arrived in Athens feeling optimistic and full of the joys of youth and travel, a military dictatorship was hard to grasp, or the fact you could be arrested for nothing more than humming the theme tune to the film *Zorba the Greek* on a city bus and then dragged off to an island gulag. Even though I was living in Athens near the end of the junta's time in Greece, as the months passed I couldn't fail to see the degree of threat and difficulty the regime brought, though not from a corner table in Zonars perhaps, pecking at a slice of custardy *galaktoboureko*.

I twice witnessed beatings and violence on the streets, and once had a lucky escape from an imminent arrest when a petulant expat friend started a mini-riot on a side street with a group of Athenians. The real impact of the junta was most apparent in those I worked for and Greeks I befriended. Nikos, my employer in Halandri, had lost his job on a city newspaper due to his political allegiances and he never worked again. I was warned by Nikos and well-meaning Greek friends that even though foreigners were in less danger, I'd be wise not to go around drawing attention to my foreignness, in case I was taken for an American, as they were hated for the CIA's alleged involvement in the 1967 coup and for formally recognising the dictatorship in 1970.

I was told to dress down, be invisible but not scruffy, lest I be taken for a student.

In my first winter months I wore a long black coat I'd bought in Harrods at great expense before leaving London for Greece, a black jumper, jeans and desert boots, with my auburn hair cut short. And that was how I slunk about Athens on my own, like a shadow. No-one ever bothered me, not even in the men-only *kafeneia,* which were fascinating to me for their authenticity and, usually harmless, machismo. Here grizzled characters sat all day over board games, drinking ouzo or *tsipouro*, their arses twitching over the state of Greece.

One evening a week I taught a wealthy Greek widow, keen on improving her English conversation skills. It never felt like work as we sat in her comfortable penthouse apartment with a view of the Parthenon in the distance. Over coffee and cake, we talked about everything and anything. She often worried about me going home late on the train and one night, with demonstrations in the city, she ordered and paid for a taxi home for me.

I also taught two children twice a week: Vassilis, 10, and his sister Myrto, 8, who lived with their parents in an old-style apartment in the centre of Thissio. These lessons were always a source of normality and levity for me. The kids were sweet-natured and respectful and called me 'Miss Marjory', which seemed comically and overly attentive. Despite my pleas, they wouldn't drop the honorific 'Miss'. When I took the job on, however, I had no idea the lessons would stretch my ingenuity to its limit and topple the idea that kids absorb words like a parched summer garden sucks up the rain.

Their mother, Aliki, worked two mornings a week in a local shop and two hours after the siesta, from 6pm. These were the evenings I gave lessons. Aliki spoke some English herself and had given the kids some basic instruction, but she wanted them to learn the language from scratch from a native English speaker. She thought this would impart a better level of language skills – even though I had only high school qualifications and my accent was mildly Australian, not the clipped Home Counties accent that was more sought after among discerning Athenian matrons. I suspected the gig had more to do with childminding than English.

Aliki would wait until I arrived and then leave me in the apartment with the kids. My generous payment was left on the kitchen table, with a freshly baked cake for us to eat at the end of the lesson. I loved teaching those kids. They were stoical little mites and despite a day at school until 2pm, then home for lunch and a quick siesta, here they were learning English. Sometimes they looked sleepy and they didn't seem to be taking anything in. I had very basic Greek, they had less English, and my method was rather simple, teaching them from the old-fashioned English kids' story books which were popular in Britain. I found some in an Athens bookstore: nice stories of English rural life, country lanes, cats and horses, gymkhanas, featuring well brought up youngsters who said things like "I'm frightfully tired" and "jolly good" – a world away from Athens.

It was great fun but it wasn't easy explaining rudiments of English grammar in my rudimentary Greek. The Greek English/English Greek dictionary became my trusted friend to explain words, and the rest we did parrot fashion, repeating words and phrases over and over from the books. Mostly we muddled along and the kids seemed to find it entertaining enough. And the cake and lemonade later lured us forward. Yet what they really understood of the stories of young Oliver and Cynthia in their Sussex idyll, with their horses and county fairs, was another matter.

A few months after I'd started, Aliki wanted to talk to me before she left for work. I felt apprehensive, with good reason. She said the kids were happy with my methods, and while they could read, slowly, and understand very simple sentences or explanations in spoken English, she was concerned they couldn't engage in any kind of chat in English and could hardly make a decent sentence on their own without a lot of prompting on her part.

"Ah well, they're so young and it takes time," I assured her, but she didn't seem convinced with that so I promised I'd search out other books in the larger Athens bookstores that would help more with the grammar, although there was a dearth of such books I'd found.

"Okay, if you think that will help," she said.

Actually, by then I realised it probably wouldn't. I could see that by muddling along with the books I had, with the idle chatter and endless parrot repetitions, it would probably take about five years to have even a simple conversation with Vassilis and Myrto. Weeks later, things were pretty much the same and although the kids seemed generally happy with their lessons, I thought I'd lose the job in the end – unless, as I suspected, Aliki needed a babysitter more than an English teacher.

It was now spring and with the days being longer I was allowed to take the kids now and then to a tiny local park for part of the lesson. One day I'd had a particularly exhausting time of it, trying to get the kids to grasp a particular rural tale about a ginger cat called Peaches, which Vassilis pronounced 'Pitch*ee*s' and Myrto couldn't manage to say at all, but giggled every time she heard the word. It was a simple story but I sensed they were just tired. At least the word 'cat' had stuck.

I decided to take them to the park for a break before it got dark. We didn't speak English much, we just walked around in the waning light. The kids seemed more relaxed outside, though I was more guarded, as I increasingly was in Athens the more I got the measure of the junta's activities. The previous week, on my way home from visiting some Greek friends in the city, I was about to take a shortcut to the train station down a quiet side street. I saw a police car parked halfway down, with a man bent backwards over the bonnet and an officer punching him repeatedly. The victim was moaning loudly. I stepped into a darkened doorway to think what to do. I didn't dare continue down the street now I'd seen the attack. I might be arrested on some petty charge. So I stepped out and retreated quietly back the way I'd come.

It was one of the more disturbing things I'd experienced and it pulled me up sharply because up to that point much of the junta's thuggery had been hidden from view. Nikos had told me one day at the house in Halandri that there was a prison not far from us where mostly left-wing militants were held and tortured. If I listened carefully while lying in my bed late at night, he said, I'd hear their deathly screams. Nikos was a maverick character and a wind-up merchant and I never knew whether he'd fabricated this story to scare me or whether it really was true. Once he'd mentioned the prison, of course, I *did* hear some strange noises late at night that kept me awake. It was either true what Nikos had said, or else just a frenzied cat fight. But on that Athens side street, seeing some guy being beat up, whether he deserved it or not, was proof that all was not well in the city.

In the park with Vassilis and Myrto, we trailed along one side of it, where there were old-style houses across a narrow street. Vassilis suddenly stopped and looked towards one of the single-story homes. He seemed to be gabbling, "Pitchees, Pitchees!"

"What are you saying, Vassili?"

He scrunched up his little face and rubbed his forehead with the heel of his hand, as if mentally constipated. He pointed vibrantly at the house again, where a fat ginger cat was stalking the ancient pantiles.

Slowly and confidently, Vassilis said, "Look, Miss Marjory, jolly good cat on roof. Pitchees!"

Stunned, I wheeled round and stared at him. "Did you just speak in English, Vassili?" Or had I imagined it?

"Yes, Miss Marjory," he said, looking dazed.

"Say it again, Vassili, please," I asked, just to make sure.

He slowly repeated the sentence. I punched the air with joy. All that hard work had paid off. Okay, the sentence wasn't quite complete but the 'jolly good cat' made up for it.

"By God, I think you've got it!" I squealed, like some doolally Henry Higgins from *My Fair Lady* at the end of his tether trying to teach cockney flower seller Eliza Doolittle how to speak poncy English.

I even bent down and kissed him on the cheek. He winced. Poor Myrto looked confused. Clearly her English was lagging. Vassilis clammed up, suddenly not keen to extend the dialogue. Was it just a one-sentence fluke? I'd have to probe a bit.

"Vassili, tell me, what is the cat on that roof called, and whose cat is it?" I asked, narrowing my eyes at him.

He thought for a while, his head slung low, observing his feet, sighing loudly. Ah, ha, just as I thought. A fluke. Moments passed, then he looked up, his face beaming.

"The cat is Pitchees, Miss Marjory. He is cat of Olive and Sinth." Okay, I let the names go. His version was cute. But mission accomplished! Vassilis was really speaking English.

"Jolly good show!" I brayed as we headed home for cake and lemonade.

When Aliki returned from work, I was fizzing with excitement and made Vassilis run through the set piece of Pitchees on the old roof, thinking how impressed she'd be. Aliki smiled and patted me on the arm and Vassilis on his head, but I sensed that behind her smiley eyes she was thinking something like: *Is that all my boy can say after all these months? And who names a cat after a fruit? Ach, the English!*

Nevertheless, it was the start of more little sentences inspired by happy rural stories from the Home Counties. Even now I can clearly remember those kids and I often think about the scene in the park, wondering if somewhere in Athens today there's a couple of grown-ups who can talk with great aplomb about cats on barn roofs, or jolly good horses collecting rosettes, or how to make lemon cordial and spotted dick, probably with the residual trace of an Aussie accent.

Notwithstanding the terrible political repression of those times, and the tortures and deaths, life in other ways seemed simpler in Greece then, as it had been in 1950s Britain. There was a pleasing innocence about it, from a foreigner's perspective at least, particularly in the years following the fall of the junta. Life became more laid-back and typically pared down, comfortable, cohesive, and inclusive – before we ever started to hear that word. And it included foreigners. Many times in those early years and the following decade I had found myself, and friends I'd travelled with, wrapped up in the warm embrace of Greekness and their sense of hospitality, or *filoxenia* (love of the stranger or foreigner). As my friend Artemios in Santorini had said, "Once you've have a meal with a Greek, you're friends for life." Simple as that.

In some ways Greeks still adhere to this philosophy, but Greeks now are somewhat different from the ones I first met in the 1970s and 80s. How could it be otherwise? The world has moved on, and so have they. Most people are happy to pay homage to the past after all, but not everyone wants to live in it. Greeks have bigger aspirations now, just like everyone else, and the country is not simply a folk museum or theme park, cluttered with statues and Doric columns, or with racks of worry beads and miniature bottles of ouzo. It has become modern and European – apart from the plumbing, which remains resolutely antique, stuck with its narrow-gauge pipes and loo-paper bins! And, inevitably, many of the old cultural elements are changing or disappearing. Fewer rural Greeks wear traditional clothing now, except on national occasions. There are fewer traditional *kafeneia* and *ouzeries* in villages, and it's rare to find a working *pantopoleio*, the crammed general store which always used to smell like the musty undersides of mice, with shelves groaning under hessian bags of dried beans and lentils, desiccated bunches of mountain tea, and every other thing under the sun.

Yet old Greece, the one that existed before the EU decided to squeeze the country into a frigid northern template during the economic crisis, is still what feeds western travellers' fantasies of this bewitching country – unless they're young and hungry only for the happy-hour bars of touristy islands.

I count myself lucky that I was one of those foreigners who was able to work in and travel the length and breadth of this country in earlier decades, particularly when it was charmingly unique, before it began to change forever. Athens will always have a special place in my heart because it was the start of my love affair with Greece and its people and their maverick souls, encapsulated in the exuberant character of Zorba (created by Nikos Kazantzakis) who, in the book of the same name, promulgated the idea that 'a man needs a little madness in his life'. So do countries, now and then: a little madness to go with the spreadsheets and the clock-watching of the developed West.

Every time I've returned to Greece, I've felt that familiar pull towards Athens, even though over the years I've also girned to myself over its creeping modernism and Europe-anism. In 2012, at the height of the crisis, I was sad to see a defeated kind of Athens, mired in debt, its inhabitants stressed and punch-drunk by an endless cycle of swingeing austerity measures. And again a few years later I saw snatches of the same thing before Greece was completely through the crisis. Yet for me the disasters or failures of the city, or indeed the whole of the country, never detract from its virtues.

In the end, what Greece offers you – apart from the ancient back story of our Western civilisation – is the human touch, which you can struggle to find now in other corners of the world.

10

Athens 2017

IN a narrow street in the Plaka area of Athens, with the Acropolis as a backdrop, Jim and I saw the kind of feisty attitude we'd come to know well during our years in southern Greece. Outside a popular taverna a policeman was writing a ticket for an idiotic piece of parking. The car was right across the corner of the pavement, blocking the way for pedestrians. Not a rare event in Greece.

There was a spirited exchange after the woman driver came flapping out of a nearby shop like an aggravated chicken. You could tell she was ready to spar with the young cop (not a traffic warden but a fully equipped cop with *astinomia*, police, written on his jacket). She had a stream of excuses for the perilous parking – but he wasn't having any of it. The parking, he told her, was illegal, and that was that. She yelled back at him. He told her not to shout. She kept it up and I was impressed with this bolshy verbal attack. You don't see it often in Britain, where you'd probably be arrested for causing an affray, and it certainly wouldn't have happened during Greece's junta years of the 1970s. She'd have been whisked away and sent off to an island gulag for behavioural reassignment.

The altercation was so diverting that people began to mill about, watching. Outside diners stopped eating to lug into the dispute, which went on long after the parking ticket was written and handed over with a flourish. It was a typical kind of Greek outburst in a way: the inability to accept a rule, no matter how justified it was. "Greeks don't do rules" is a common confession in that country.

But the woman's strop in Plaka showed more than just a dislike of rules. It was part of a collective irritation we'd seen creeping into Greek life from around 2012, with ongoing austerity and the consequences of the crisis: unemployment, hunger, lack of medical services, rising suicide rates. The crisis had slowly become a humanitarian disaster. In 2017 the streets of downtown Athens had a neglected aura about them, with graffiti sprayed over buildings, and while some of it was an arty emblem of the recent troubles (and still is), in other cases it was downright ugly, especially scrawled on old neo-classical houses in Plaka. What seemed most distressing was the number of older women we saw begging. One woman was camped on the edge of a pavement, holding a sign saying, "I am a Greek woman and I am living in poverty. Help me!"

We heard tales of stress and frustration, from shopkeepers and from friends who live and work in Athens, that the crisis had hammered their businesses, with endless taxes. I told an Athenian businessman and friend when we met him for lunch that we'd just read reports in British papers that the Greek economy was finally improving and 'turning a corner'. "Pah!" he said vibrantly. "Turning a corner yes, but into a *gremos* (ravine)!"

My friend's darkly comical point made me reflect again on my first year-long stay in Athens in the 1970s. This was another perilous era in the city's history, as I wrote in the previous chapter, yet the years since the start of Greece's economic crisis seemed somehow more hopeless. You can get rid of a regime in the end, but an economic crisis can go on forever, and take the country down to a new level. Another friend in Athens, who works as an economist, told me that although the country was in better shape than previously in the crisis, and had managed to repay some of its huge debt and carry out economic restructuring, she believed the Greek debt would never fully be paid off. The debt would be kicked on down the road by successive governments so that the next generation would have to deal with it.

With or without a crisis, Athens has changed, of course. It's not quite the place I discovered in the 1970s, but then neither is London or Paris. The old sectors like Plaka, Monastiraki and Thissio that I knew well and loved seemed down at heel in 2017, despite a gentrifying of these quarters in the past few decades. In the past they had buzzed – full of authentic tavernas, arty jewellery shops with unique folky designs, galleries, stalls belonging to local craftsmen – and were easy, peaceful places to navigate. A few galleries and arty shops remained but much of the old neighbourhoods now seemed to be dominated by a slew of outlets selling cheap goods, mostly made in India and China. And competition seemed fierce.

Along a narrow street in Monastiraki, I passed a gaudy souvenir shop where the old crone of a proprietor was standing outside, spruiking her trinkets in passable English. She had a funny turn and latched on to my hand, with the pretence of a welcoming handshake, and tried to haul me into her cluttered lair, like a ravenous spider. She was strong. I couldn't shake her off. At the door of the shop, with Jim further up the street and oblivious to my plight, I became anxious. Was I about to disappear forever among the statues of Apollo with oversized penises, the plaster Parthenons and the rows of sun-faded blue-and-white cheesecloth shirts circa 1969? I couldn't tug my hand away so I dug in my heels and shouted rather dramatically, "Let me go, please!" Passers-by stopped and gawped – witnesses to my abduction. She finally let go of me.

"Have you gone completely mad?" I sniped at her. Without waiting for a response, I skittered up the road towards Jim.

"Where have you been? I nearly got kidnapped back there!" I said when I caught up with him.

"Huh?" he replied vaguely, his head full of something else. Not much, as it turned out. He opened a plastic bag to show me a navy T-shirt that said *Limeniko Soma,* Greek coastguard, with an official-looking badge.

"So, you've joined the coastguard?"

"Don't be daft," he chuckled. "I've just bought this. It's great, eh? But I can't wear it in Greece. The shopkeeper told me that's illegal. And the Greek *Astinomia,* police T-shirt, especially that one, but it's apparently pretty popular too. I might go back for that one another time." On and on he trilled like a Village People anorak. He wasn't the least bit interested in my battle with the crone.

"Oh go on, buy a police T-shirt to wear around Athens. Break a few rules!" I said, with a smirk.

"You're having a laugh, aren't you?" he said, frowning. He stuffed the T-shirt back in the bag.

So not everything in Monastiraki is without interest these days. The flea market in this area still lures punters. Like a frenetic version of Steptoe and Son's junkyard, without the knackered horse and cart, it teems with narrow shops filled with piles of old stuff that looks like everything you've ever tried to sell at a car boot sale but failed. It's not like the old market I remember, but it has its charm and interestingly, amid the emporiums of junk, there are still a few workers toiling away at traditional crafts. We saw two guys with hands like grappling irons repairing rush-bottomed chairs with lengths of dried rushes. It brought back old images of a time when men sat by pop-up stalls creating leather goods.

Part of what has been lost in the old neighbourhoods like Plaka are the vibrant tavernas, *kafeneia* and ouzeries that had their heyday in the 1950s and 60s, when the area was the coolest place to socialise. Tavernas were rustic retreats back then, serving retsina from wine barrels, and locals often gathered late at night to sing *kantades,* serenades, that were more popularly thought of as 'wine songs'. Smoky bars and nightclubs played popular *laiki* music and *rebetika* (Greek blues) brought to Greece by exiles from Asia Minor. This was also the era of the wonderful *koutoukia*, basement tavernas, with a Turkish influence, coming from the Turkish word *kutuk,* meaning 'familiar'. They offered simple fare, music, and in the edgier, male-only dens, illegal substances.

They remained popular in the 1970s and I remember them as some of the best places to spend a convivial evening with friends over a carafe of wine from the barrels that lined the walls. They were frequented by artists, students, musicians, and of course the bouzouki players and singers. In the 70s, during the junta, their slightly hidden basement location made them perfect places for the dispossessed of the era to meet and sing banned songs and decry the regime, all of which was illegal. There are a few of the *koutoukia* still in Athens, I'm told, but you'd have to hunt them down. From the 1970s into the 80s loud music was outlawed in the Plaka, bringing an end the more vibrant tavernas and nightclubs, which were moved on to edgier neighbourhoods like Psiri and Thissio, which is why today Plaka has fewer restaurants that feel as authentic as they used to.

Some of the shopkeepers in Athens we spoke to in 2017 lamented the fact the area wasn't what it used to be in recent decades. One taverna owner told us, "The old neighbourhood's finished. The 'real' people were moved on by the city's bureaucratic planners to make way for the renovation of the old Plaka houses." These same houses, with their beautiful stone work and fabulous courtyards, now have to dodge the graffiti artist's spray can.

However, what has happened to the old neighbourhoods of central Athens, with its great characters and vibrant heart, has happened in most cities in the world. And it could be said there's little virtue in trying to conjure up the glorious past. It's a bit like blowing hot air into long-dead Tutankhamen.

In Thissio one day I looked for the old apartment where I'd once taught the two children, Vassilis and Myrto, as if I might still find them there, middle-aged now, their grandchildren perhaps mulling over the dog-eared English books I'd left them with, reading about 'Pitchees' the cat. But the building had been replaced by something newer and flashier. The park where Vassilis uttered his first proper English sentence, as I mentioned in the previous chapter, was no longer there, even though there was much still to like about the quieter nooks and crannies of this quarter.

But the city neighbourhoods offer something unique, no matter what the era, and a stunning amount of treasures from different periods of history that sit cheek by jowl with modern layers, like a kind of geological core sample turned on its side. Wandering there today, you'll find impressive ancient sites like the 2nd century BC Tower of the Winds, once a Roman meteorological station with a sundial on its splendid hexagonal tower, along with Byzantine churches with curious histories, monuments, remnants of old monasteries and renovated neo-classical houses.

Other places in Athens only vaguely evoke past charm. In Syntagma Square one day, on the way to the Metro, I looked over the vast expanse of the square full of people scurrying home and beggars camped in their own patch of misery in the crisis. I remembered how elegant it used to be in the 1970s, with its rows of café tables and chairs at the bottom, near Ermou Street, and how the waiters would run the gauntlet from the cafés nearby, crossing the roads with laden trays. One of the most indelible TV images I have of Syntagma from the crisis years is the huge industrial garbage bins set on fire one night by protesters bitterly opposing more austerity. The black-clad youngsters were running a different kind of gauntlet on the road outside the Parliament building, launching these fiery missiles while police teams tore into action, gathering up the suspects.

But central Athens still has a warm community heart, and you can see many examples of it. From the dining room of our hotel on the edge of Plaka, I caught a glimpse each day of a pop-up coffee shop across the road. It was nothing more than a tiny outlet on a wedge of pavement beside an apartment block, with a couple of tables outside. Every morning a handful of locals, of different ages, would gather to shoot the breeze and have a laugh over tiny cups of Greek coffee. It was a nice scene and I enjoyed the conviviality of their lives, despite the gloom of their economics.

I end my reflections on Athens by returning to the Acropolis because over the decades it has lured me like the mythological Sirens on the rocks. The name means 'city at the top' and is referred to by the Greeks as the 'holy rock' because from Neolithic times it has always had religious significance. The Parthenon was commissioned by the statesman Pericles in the 5th century BC as a temple, dedicated to the goddess Athena. It is still majestic despite being hammered over the centuries by earthquakes, sieges, and explosions when the Ottoman Turks turned it into a garrison and took their target practice there. And it is still outstandingly beautiful even without its original statues and carved marble panels, the 'Marbles', of its outer facades that Lord Elgin plundered in the 19th century.

In the 1970s there was always a thread of heated discussion in the city about the erosion of the exquisite Pendeli marble of the Parthenon and the nearby smaller temples. It was the fault of the foul *nefos*, the smog, in the city from dilapidated cars and poor traffic control. Yet the buildings are still standing and haven't dissolved in the acid bath of pollution. It's to the credit of the Greeks, and perhaps to some of the EU grants, that the Acropolis buildings and their antiquities have been lovingly restored and maintained.

And for a country that doesn't like rules, the rules applying to the Acropolis are stern, and often rather comical. Tourists are probably the latest scourge to replace pollution. Greek guards on the Acropolis do their best to keep tourists from ruining the buildings and the environment. Naturally, taking small marble souvenirs is outlawed, as is touching and groping the antiquities. When we visited in 2017 there was a list of rules displayed at the foot of the Acropolis. It was illegal to make videos on the rock without permission; to take "improper photos" (whatever they may be) and also to "sing and make a loud noise" or to "introduce food or animals into the Acropolis". So if you were planning to take your dog up there and sing an aria over a quick takeaway souvlaki, you'd have no luck. And the attendants patrolling the site mean business. Near the Parthenon the sight of one young visitor languishing on a bench of marble for a cute photo opportunity brought an attendant with big Medusa hair flying out of her security hut, waving her arms and admonishing the poor soul in front of a swarm of visitors. He'll never do that again.

Whenever I'm in Athens, I always visit the Acropolis. I sit on the low south-facing wall beside the Parthenon, overlooking the Herodes Atticus theatre, built down the steep side of the rock in 161 AD by the Romans. Beyond it, the southern flank of the city is spread out all the way to the Saronic Gulf.

It feels like the most beautiful and culturally significant place to be, perhaps anywhere in the world, and it's easy to see why the Greeks still love the Parthenon so much. Like a seasoned and unadorned heroine in an ancient Greek tragedy, it has become an enduring symbol also for grace, and survival, the Greek talent for rising above the transient flow of historic catastrophes. Like this temple, the country has withstood the worst of troubles: foreign occupations, wars, juntas, earthquakes, starvation and economic collapse – as well as the eternal cheesecloth shirts of Monastiraki, and the image of Demis Roussos singing in kaftans.

(For more about the Parthenon, read Chapter 18 on the Elgin Marbles and a surprising modern-day Scottish connection.)

11

Crete expectations

I'VE never enjoyed media events on boats. For a start, if the function proves to be a terrible bore you can't escape very easily. In November 1990 I found myself on a boat sailing about Thessaloniki harbour in northern Greece with a media contingent and the city's mayor and dignitaries. It was a glorious setting: the waters of the Thermaic Gulf were calm, with a sunset glimmer of red and gold over them, and the city was spread out along the waterfront and up into the low hills behind. Perfect.

However, halfway through the evening, while everyone was eating canapes and quaffing champagne, I was below deck in the toilet, being sick. The culprit: prawns. Not that anything the mayor served up for the visiting media was off – far from it. But prawns had become my temporary nemesis in a long sojourn in Greece that had begun nearly two months earlier on the island of Crete and proved to me the wisdom of the Greek saying, "When man makes plans, God laughs!"

It all started in the latter part of 1990 when the Sydney newspaper I worked for as a feature writer offered me a media trip to Greece, one of the wonderful perks of journalism. Of course I was eager to go. It was around 10 days' long, starting with a few days in Athens and then a flight to Thessaloniki to cover an autumn travel conference and to visit the attractions of this unique northern city. However, I contrived to turn it into a longer trip by changing the date of my outward-bound flight and tacking on to the front of the media trip six weeks of holidays that I'd accrued over a few years, which had to be taken. No hardship, of course! So here I was having a kind of sabbatical in Greece, the first trip there for a few years. I planned a week in Athens to enjoy some favourite hangouts with a few old friends before sailing to Crete, where I'd spent some time in the 1970s after finishing up a year's work stint in Athens.

I took a ferry to Hania, the pretty Venetian town in the north-west of Crete, and checked into a harbourside hotel. The town still retained much of its charm from earlier decades despite the addition of modern shops and bars from the increase of cheap flights and mass tourism. I took a room at the front of the hotel with a protruding Venetian-style balcony offering stunning harbour views. I also made some short excursions by bus around the west of the island and to the village of Hora Sfakion on the south coast. It was from here that around 15,000 allies were evacuated after the German occupation of Crete in World War Two, many having walked over the White Mountains and through the nearby Imbros Gorge to reach the village.

My final excursion was a sentimental journey back to a tiny coastal settlement a few miles west of Hania, where I'd stayed for a few months in the 70s. I'd been offered a modest stone house by an Athenian friend. It was in an idyllic location, opposite the sea and surrounded by olive groves. It was a basic summer house, with no hot water and no proper heating, apart from a smoky oil heater. The area had been wonderfully raw in those days, traditional, full of generous and outlandish characters, who frequented the few tavernas that dotted the quiet shoreline. They were sociable places and often lively, like the popular Keratas taverna, meaning Cuckold.

I took a bus to the coastal village to see what the area was like now after so many years. I asked the driver to let me know when we got to a particular junction where the summer house was situated and where a side road wound up towards the mountain range behind. When he stopped the bus to let me off, I thought he must have made a mistake. I stood on the side of the road feeling shocked because I didn't recognise this place at all. It was a travesty of the traditional village it used to be. The road by the sea was built up on both sides: an ugly sprawl of cafés, mini-markets and tourist shops crammed in as far as the eye could see. The once quiet beach was packed with sunbeds, and the few tavernas I'd remembered were no more. Certainly not the Keratas. Nothing resembled the untouched spot it used to be. Had it not been for the side road to the mountains I might have thought I was somewhere else entirely.

And on the corner of the side road, where the stone house had stood, there was no trace of it. I felt my eyes sting with tears when I saw an ugly mini-market with the usual tat out front: flippers, garish beach towels, dog-eared magazines. Depressed with the vision before me, I got on the next bus heading back to town, thinking I'd have to get over the fact that since the 1970s rural Crete had changed and developed more than anyone might have expected, like much of the rest of Greece.

I spent some enjoyable days, however, exploring the narrow Venetian alleyways of Hania, and the town's hinterland, with no onward plans. For a while at least I'd be Greek and live day by day. What I didn't envisage was that I'd suddenly get sick, not something that has happened much in Greece. A meal at a nearby restaurant – barbecued king prawns! – gave me a bad stomach bug that floored me for several days, my only distraction being the small top-floor balcony off my hotel room that seemed like an opera box now as I slumped at the metal table, staring pale and sickly at the frenetic goings-on below: the holidaymakers, the hawkers, the hustlers, the characters, like the old guy with his flat-bed truck selling every kind of nut, laid out in trays, and talking loudly with every other kind of nut who stopped by. When he wasn't talking, he was smoking, or listening to an old transistor radio clamped to his ear, with Greek music or sports commentary turned up to the max. Yet it passed the time for both of us.

I imagined that to the people scurrying about below who chanced to look up at me, staring over the metal railing, I must have resembled a bit of a nut myself, a tormented theatre-goer at La Scala having the vapours over some dramatic coup de grace in the opera plot. Some of the local café and taverna owners became used to the sight of me and waved sporadically, though not the owner of the taverna whose prawns laid me low. No, I never saw him at all.

Day after day, I felt like I was losing the plot, operatic or otherwise, with my health and a doctor was finally summoned, medicines administered, and a strict diet recommended. No olive oil for a while, fried food or booze. Ah, the joys of the sabbatical –and I still had many weeks to go. I sent a note to one of the tavernas below asking if they could send me up some simple dishes each day, and they duly arrived on a tray carried by the owner's young son, with little treats on the side: yoghurt with honey and slices of baklava.

When I started to recover I decided to move away from anything resembling memory lane because it's a location that, as I've often found, will yield endless disappointments. I would go to the other side of the island, which I'd only visited briefly in the 70s. A chance recommendation from a fellow Aussie I'd met in the town made me seek out a convalescence of sorts in the fishing village of Elounda, in the north-east, on the Bay of Mirabello. Why I fixed on it I have no idea, but when you travel alone you become victim to strange whims, and just the sound of a place can act like a strong lure.

The Aussie contact made it sound appealing: a fishing village in an undeveloped area – as it was then – with the addition of the curious island called Spinalonga, which was once a leper colony, now deserted. This was long before Victoria Hislop cleverly featured the location in her best-selling novel, *The Island*, and tourist boats began to take visitors there in their thousands.

So that was a plan of sorts. I felt somewhat revived, but had no stomach for a ride in one of those old bone-rattler buses, where locals squeeze in with cans of olive oil, chickens in boxes, lots of noise, arguing and smoking. I wanted to get to the destination quickly, so I splashed out and took a taxi. When I told the driver I was going to Elounda, a long drive from Hania, his eyebrows pinged up with delight. A good day's work for him.

When he pulled up at Elounda harbour I felt instantly uplifted.

"You see how lovely it is," said the driver, who had hardly spoken for the last hour or so but smoked incessantly. "Traditional place, lots of nice boats. And look, the mountains behind. Very lovely."

Indeed, the village had a soothing traditional quality about it, the little square with its domed church, the low-key cafés and tavernas, pointy Mount Oxa looming behind like a pyramid. And the bay, stretching from the village to the north between the mainland and the opposite peninsula, was soft and still in the afternoon heat. This would do me.

The taxi driver asked where I was staying. I shrugged. "Nothing booked."

He shrugged back. "Not a problem."

Everything would be fine, he intimated, despite it being early October, with some hotels due to close for winter, as well as tavernas. These were the days when the tourist season was shorter than it is now. The cabbie cruised about the harbour, looking for a sign for rooms to rent. At a row of two-storey apartment blocks opposite the beach, he stopped for a moment to ponder his next move. There were no signs anywhere but some instinct must have got the better of him and after a while a short, smiley woman barrelled down a path to her front gate.

"Are you looking for rooms?" she asked.

I nodded. The driver stayed in the cab while I went to look at what was on offer. It was a ground-floor flat, with a large bedroom/sitting room, a bathroom and small kitchen diner.

We talked about money. It was cheap.

"I'll take it, for four weeks or so," I said.

The woman looked pleasantly surprised, and that was that. The taxi driver took in my suitcase. I gave him a healthy tip and he handed me his business card, in case I needed a lift again, or if I needed anything at all. He squeezed my arm in an avuncular fashion.

It was the start of a wonderful stay in Elounda, and a friendship with the couple upstairs, Polina and Kostas, who owned the flat. Greek friendships never start slowly. Mostly they go at a gallop from the starters' gate if the people like you and trust you. Polina often sat with me outside the front door of the flat, where a small table and chairs had been set, to chat about the village, her family, but mostly about me: How old? Married? Children? House? How much? The usual bold things that Greeks ask of strangers. She was bemused by my sabbatical.

"You're going to Thessaloniki in November? *Po, po, po!*" she said, the Greek equivalent of 'bloody hell!', with a wave of her chubby brown hand. "Cold up there, very far. Better to stay here."

She was also bemused by my prawn malady. "Yes, you look a bit pale and thin," she said, adding, "A Greek saying goes, 'if you don't trust the fisherman, don't trust the prawn'." Or words to that affect. I knew what she meant. Polina mostly spoke very adequate English in her colourful fashion but also let me chatter away sometimes in my rusty Greek for practice.

During the day, I rambled about the village and took short bus trips around the area and up to the mountain villages. I walked to the peninsula opposite, called Kalydon, which was joined to the mainland by a narrow isthmus. In the evenings, Polina often invited me upstairs to her apartment to watch TV, while Kostas was at the *kafeneio* with his friends, or out fishing, which he did a lot from his small boat, the Peristeri. We watched Greek soaps on TV, which I didn't understand much.

Polina sometimes took me rambling up on the hills behind Elounda. Back then there wasn't much on the hillside except olive groves and a few stone windmills at the top. Now and then we collected *horta*, the wild greens that Greek women have great expertise in winkling out of dried rocky hillsides. They all looked green to me but she showed me which ones were edible and which were not. We would carry our bulging bags home and sit on her front balcony, a great pile of greens on the table in front of us, chopping off roots and preparing them to be boiled and doused in lemon and olive oil. It was hardly Happy Hour, with cocktails decked out in paper parasols, but it was a perfect way to recuperate from the prawn malady, and I felt fitter.

Polina often brought me something nice from Kostas's latest catch, but any seafood – prawns mostly – made me feel nauseous. A case of post-enteritis stress disorder, or PESD for short.

This easy-going location was just what I was looking for because I knew that once I got back to Athens, and then Thessaloniki, the media gig would be non-stop events and tours, as they always are. However, after a week in Elounda I felt there was only so much bucolic bliss I could take, even in Crete. And Polina too began to fret. "You not lonely here with just a few Greeks for company?" I wasn't and I knew that when the day came and I needed some other kind of conversation that didn't include wild dandelions, fishing, Greek soaps and so forth, I would come across company somewhere because in my experience Greece is the kind of place where people find you, not the other way round – whether you want it or not.

With the weather still wonderfully warm for autumn, I swam daily at the village beach across the road, which was usually near-deserted. One morning a young guy turned up and sat on his towel near me at the edge of the water. I got up and went for a long swim. A sea breeze was picking up, which made the water feel a bit cooler. After a long swim up the edge of the bay, I felt invigorated and turned and swam quickly back. When I got out of the water, the guy looked up, narrowing his eyes. I dried off and sat on my towel, enjoying the hot sun.

"Do you mind my asking, is the water very cold?" he said, in a southern English accent.

"It's a bit cool at first, but fine otherwise."

"Ah," he said with a pout. "Cool is the same as cold to me. I never usually come to places like Greece outside high summer."

Then why was he here, I wondered?

"All you Pommies hate cold water," I said with a light smirk, using the nickname that Aussies use for the English. I'd seen British tourists on countless Greek beaches, even in the middle of summer, their shoulders hunched up to their ears, screaming comically when the tide lapped over their knees. It was clear this guy was dithering over a swim but didn't want to look like a wimp.

"Go on, it won't kill you. This thing about cold water, it's all in the mind," I said, touching my forehead.

He smiled. "You're Australian, aren't you? I would have thought you wouldn't like anything that was colder than warm bath water. Isn't it always like that over there? Not that I've been yet, I have to say."

"Not always. In spring the Pacific Ocean's what I would call pretty cold before it warms up but you get used to it. Australians are pretty fearless anyway." Unlike the British migrants in Australia, who always wait until the water's jacuzzi warm.

The young guy finally got up, walked to the edge of the water, rubbing his arms and wincing. He crept in, his shoulders massaging his ears, though it really wasn't that cold. I stifled a guffaw as he dived in with a roar of discomfort, as if he was having a dip in the Arctic. He then swam a plodding freestyle for a few metres. Promptly, he turned and swam back, then sprinted to his towel to dry himself.

"That wasn't so bad, was it?" I asked.

"Bloody cold actually."

"Come on! That is not cold. In southern Greece people swim till Christmas."

He sat on his towel, looking a bit shamefaced. "You must think I've never done this before."

"What, swim in October? Or confess your temperature phobia to a stranger on the beach?" I quipped cheekily.

He laughed. "Both."

I had a sense this guy had never done anything outside his comfort zone before. Poor lamb.

We sat in silence for a while, enjoying the sunshine, the sight of the bay spread out before us. He was a nice-looking guy, a bit younger than me, with a warm smile, thick light brown hair, slightly wavy. He was affable without being creepy or flirty. Not as flirty as I seemed to be. It was a pity I was in no way looking for a senseless holiday romance while on the rebound from a tormenting relationship in Sydney, which had been one of the reasons for this sabbatical, if not the major one.

"Is this your first trip to Crete?" I asked him.

He nodded and then I heard his story, which cleared up the matter of a possible holiday romance. Even when people don't know what I do for a living, for some strange reason they have an urge to tell me their story, even with only the slightest of prompting, which is often entertaining. But when they know I'm a journalist it's a different matter. I either get no conversation at all, or the opposite, a tale pumped up to the max, usually a tormenting one. I sometimes think journalists are nothing but psychiatrists without the couch and the inflated fees.

His name was Joseph. He'd come to Elounda to meet up with a married woman he'd been having a long, passionate affair with. She'd finally split from her husband. All very messy. The old story. However, she'd suddenly decided to take off on a jaunt to Italy and Greece – a kind of stress leave – to sort out her head. It had been her idea, he said, to meet up in a sunny location, to have a secret, romantic rendezvous to herald their new life together. So he'd flown out here. Why Elounda, he didn't say. It sounded very adventurous for a guy who was scared of a little cold water and seemed strangely lacking in confidence. It was all the more intriguing when he said he was the manager of an expensive boutique hotel in Edinburgh.

"Is your hotel pool heated?" I asked him.

He laughed. "Yes, it is."

"Thank God for that!" I said with exaggerated surprise, but he took it well.

Perhaps he was just feeling nervous about this forthcoming rendezvous and needed to unload his story on to a stranger. Poor guy. Poor me! But I had nothing better to do right at that minute and the tale was at least better than the histrionic storylines I'd tolerated so far on Greek TV.

"So when's your girlfriend arriving?"

"In a few days."

"That's lovely. I hope it all works out," I said, offering an encouraging smile.

"Yes, so do I. Things have been a bit emotional for a while. Stressful too, you know, keeping our affair secret. She's an interior designer. She does a lot of work for our hotel. And we both know a lot of people in the city. I've only been in Edinburgh for two years but I've learnt that although it seems like a big city it isn't really. It's on a very human scale and gossip travels. But hey, I apologise for taking up your time with this story," he smiled coyly.

"Don't worry, I'm a journalist. I hear *lots* of candid stories, all the time," I said for a bit of a wind-up.

His eyes widened. "You're not going to make notes and work all this into a newspaper feature?" he said, with a nervy lip-twitch.

"Nope. It's all up here though for later." I smirked, tapping my forehead, enjoying the moment.

There was a long beat of silence, in which I thought I'd probably gone too far, but then he laughed. Shortly after, he got up to leave, saying he had phone calls to make. He gathered his things together, shoving them into a stripy bag.

"Good luck with everything," I said with a wave, not expecting to see him again.

"Thanks. Nice to meet you," he said and walked away, then stopped and turned back.

"Em ... it's kind of quiet here in the evening now the season's drawing in. I don't suppose you'd like to join me for dinner at the taverna in the square, the only one open now, it seems. My treat. It's the least I can do for bending your ear with my love story."

"Oh, you didn't bend it much. But if you like. That would be nice," I said, surprised at his offer. I don't know why I agreed to it but it would make a change from my usual evening entertainment so far: struggling through TV soaps, or wandering alone round the harbour, watching fishermen mending nets, or tracking down backstreet *kafeneia* for a glass of wine and the chance to listen to locals bantering.

We met at 8pm in the Gorgona taverna. It was a pleasant evening. He was good company and told me more about his job as a hotel manager: funny stories about strange guests, eccentric behaviour, especially with foreigners. My favourite yarn was about an American guest dressed for a traditional Scottish evening, wearing a kilt, with the sporran (tasselled pouch) slung over his shoulder like a bag, with no sense of cultural faux pas or irony. I laughed wildly at the comical vision he painted. Joseph grew in confidence as the evening progressed.

He seemed sensible as well – far too sensible to be having a messy meet-up with a still-to-be-divorced minx. But what really piqued my interest was why his lover needed to drag him all the way to Greece for this assignation, a country he didn't seem familiar with, when a Scottish Highland bolthole might have done just as well. And he'd spared no effort and expense with a room in the Elounda Bay Palace, one of the classiest hotels built on a low headland around the corner from the village, with its own private beaches and top facilities. I imagined he dined there most nights and perhaps the suggestion of this village taverna was a concession to me. Neutral territory, and all that. But none of it was my concern.

"No doubt I'll see you around. It's a small place," he said as we wound up the evening. "Perhaps you'd like to have a meal with us some time at the Elounda Bay before we leave. It has a great terrace restaurant with a fab view. We've got a week here."

I gave him a squinty look. I imagined that after the girlfriend arrived, he'd rather retreat to his suite for a whole week of unbridled passion. I would, in his position.

"Sure. If you've got time," I said to be polite, but playing gooseberry with two love-sick puppies at a messy juncture in life wasn't my idea of fun. Anyway, I had sightseeing to do in this corner of Crete before I left, and an imminent fishing expedition.

Kostas liked to fish. Once or twice he and Polina had taken me out on their small boat, from which they would cast long nets into the bay to be collected up next morning, hopefully with a good catch. It was pleasing to sit in the boat while the couple unwound the nets into the still water, with the lights of Elounda harbour twinkling around us. The fishing expedition they planned would take about half a day to Spinalonga island. Kostas was hoping to catch squid or octopus there, as well as fish, and Polina and I would have time off to ramble over the island. It was to be a 5am start, not something I'd usually enjoy, but I've found in life that the things you never plan to do because they seem difficult or painful will have the sweetest outcomes. And the things you plan for ... well!

The couple tapped on my bedroom window well before sunrise. I had just enough time for a quick coffee and a slice of bread before we set off on Kostas's boat, moored nearby. Out on the water it was quiet and still, with a slight chill in the air. Kostas warned me to bring a jacket and I was glad of it. The couple were dressed warmly and Kostas also wore an old grey woollen balaclava, which made him look like he was on a commando mission. The boat had a small outboard motor and we cruised steadily along the bay. The sky was still dark, with just a faint bleeding of red from behind the long Kalydon peninsula, with the expanse of Mirabello Bay beyond it.

When we were close to the dark, slightly chilling form of Spinalonga island, Kostas cut the motor and dropped anchor. We sat for a while in silence, watching the sun begin its slow ascent from behind the peninsula in bands of deep red and purple, against which a solitary, slow-moving sea bird cut a dramatic path. We didn't talk. It seemed enough just to be there, to enjoy that sublime moment, sleepy from our early start. Just before 7am, when the sun was higher and the sky had lightened, Spinalonga took on a more impressive form with the walls of the medieval fortress above the old stone quay. It was superficially appealing, at least.

Kostas got to work on his long fishing line, knotted with what seemed to be dozens of hooks. He threaded a small prawn onto each one and dropped the load into the clear turquoise water. As the sun rose higher, we became more talkative, with Polina, like a smiley tour guide, giving me some history of the bay and the Spinalonga leper colony.

Kostas fussed over his fishing line, and from my seat on the starboard side, with him in front of me, I could see the line clearly and became strangely fascinating by the sight of hooks delving down into the deep, with fish beginning to impale themselves with a flash of silver through the water. Kostas waited until all the hooks were squirming and then pulled the lot up. They were all smallish fish but good for pan frying. The whole process was repeated again and again.

"It's the octopus he wants," said Polina with a wink.

After what seemed liked hours of bobbing about in the boat, hauling in fish, Kostas started up the motor and took us to the quay on the island and dropped us there. Polina had packed lunch in a basket with stout handles. Kostas told us he'd be back in an hour or so, and to be waiting for him. He didn't want to have to come and find us.

"I've seen the island," he said with a slight grimace. "Everyone in Elounda knows someone who suffered here in the old days. It's not a happy place." He seemed keen to get away and waved as he motored quietly around the side of the island towards rocks, where I guessed he was in pursuit of an elusive octopus.

We walked up from the quay into the settlement. Ahead there were narrow cobbled streets and above us the towering fortress. We sat under a shady tree and ate bread, cheese, olives and fruit. Polina told me more about the colony. Although it now draws tourists like a magnet, back then the settlement was almost unheard of outside Greece.

The island had once been a Venetian and then an Ottoman stronghold, with the fortress and stout walls for protection. In 1904 the Turks finally left the island and it was taken back by the Greeks and turned into a leper colony by 1913. Although treatments were discovered for leprosy in the 1940s, it seems the Greeks had their own leper agenda and kept the island operational until 1957, with only one doctor. It became a dark secret and was only finally liberated after a visiting British doctor discovered the unfortunate souls still living in exile.

After lunch we trailed around the streets of the settlement, admiring old houses with stout lintels on the doors and shuttered windows. There was an eerie charm about the place, especially in the 'commercial' area that had once contained cafés, a school and shops. So not everything about the island lifestyle had been drab and without comforts. Yet a wind around midday funnelled its way through the streets and stone archways and it felt cold, despite the warm sun.

When Kostas later picked us up from the quay, I was pleased to see him and to be leaving the island. Spinalonga had a dispiriting aura, as if all the fears and shattered hopes of the exiled lepers weighed heavily over it, like a leaden sky in winter. I felt my mood rise the further away we got. Kostas had a good bucket of fish and despite the lack of an octopus he was happy, and had even taken off his balaclava. We skimmed past the mainland shoreline that had previously been in darkness and I noted the start of new hotel developments I'd passed on long walks from Elounda. These would become grand five-star inclusive hotels in the years to come.

I didn't venture into the village much for a few days, as the weather had turned stormy, and I didn't expect to see Joseph again. But one morning, while I was having coffee on the outside terrace of one of the *kafeneia* still open on the main square, he walked past, deep in thought. He hadn't seen me, so I called out. He turned and gave me a vague look, as if he'd forgotten who I was. He looked tired.

"Are you alone?" I asked as he approached the table.

"Well, yes, as it happens," he said, with a light frown, which piqued my interest.

"Have a seat and tell me how things are going, if you have time," I said, thinking I sounded intrusive. But the other thing about being a journalist I've found is that while half your life you're batting away strangers' complicated tales, the other half, conversely, you feel the urge to interview almost everyone you meet. An occupational peculiarity.

He seemed edgy, looking around as if he feared someone may be listening, but then pulled up a chair and sat down.

"Sorry, I'm a bit slow today."

Heavy night, I thought. The woman sleeping it off.

He ordered a filter coffee. He spooned in some sugar and then stirred the coffee for a long time without talking. I waited, my eyebrows arching with curiosity.

"Natasha arrived three days ago. Now she's gone ... *already*," he said, shrugging massively, his palms out, like a Greek. I took a sharp intake of breath.

"Oh, do you want to talk about it?"

"There's not much to say. She'd been travelling around Italy, then Greece. She had a week in Athens – and that's where she met some guy, a Scot, as it happens. She said she's head over heels ..." He stopped, his eyes flickering towards me, as if to see how I was taking all this. I was shocked, but deep down I'd already guessed the woman was going to be a bit of a car crash. Now I saw she was a heartless coquette.

Joseph's sunglasses were pushed up on his head and I thought I saw a tinge of red in his eyes.

"So it seems she's in love, or lust, with this guy and she doesn't want to have anything to do with me now. Incredible, after me coming all this way!"

I shook my head. "That's appalling, Joseph. Poor you, but I guess she probably wasn't on the level with you from the beginning, was she? Just playing you along, and crashing into every man standing. I pity the new guy."

He nodded and scraped his top teeth over his lower lip, as if to hold back a tear. I felt sorry for him.

"But there's one good thing about it, Joseph. At least she came here and told you in person, and didn't waste time about it."

"True. She could have just rung the hotel. But I wish she had. It was awkward. When she arrived at hotel reception the first day, I was called on the phone and went down to meet her. She didn't look pleased to see me, but I really knew it was going to be a disaster when she asked to have a separate room to mine, which was hardly the plan. So we had this horrible, embarrassing discussion in front of the receptionist about why Natasha wanted a separate room. She didn't say why, right there, but kept insisting on it. So obviously I knew something had gone pear-shaped. And the irony is that I'd booked one of the best rooms in the hotel with a view of the bay. Very romantic!"

He exhaled painfully and fiddled with the spoon on his saucer, clattering it about. He gave me a mournful look.

"What a brass neck she's got! Why didn't she just go off to another hotel and leave you in peace?"

"Well, she only stayed one night. We had a tormenting dinner in the hotel while she tried to excuse the new love affair. She told me she'd be leaving first thing to get the bus to Rethymnon on the coast to see some friends, and then it was back to Athens. End of story."

Poor guy, and what a faff. I couldn't help but wonder at the trouble the girlfriend had gone to, trailing all the way to Crete to deliver the bad news to Joseph.

He was clattering his teaspoon again, staring into his cup like a Greek trying to read his future in the coffee grounds.

"Look, Joseph," I said, tapping his arm softly to get his attention. "Affairs with married people always go badly. She did you a favour showing her hand now."

"Yes, I agree, but I'm a bit shell-shocked. I didn't see any of this coming and I've known her a year. I'm pissed off with my own lack of insight." Another Greek shrug.

"I expect you'll be keen to leave Elounda now," I said.

"Well no, actually. I've changed my plans. I've contacted the hotel in Edinburgh and told them I need to stay here for another week, that I'm studying some of the new hotels that are going up ... getting some corporate ideas. I fudged it a bit, but it's fine. Right now I really need a holiday, to be honest."

Good for you, I thought.

"And, can I say, I'm grateful for your company and your input. I'd be in a worse state without it," he said, with a faltering smile.

"Oh ... Think nothing of it. I feel bad for you though."

We lapsed into silence, then he seemed to rouse himself.

"I've an idea. Let's have dinner again, at the hotel this time. The restaurant has a fab view. Might as well get my money's worth out of the place. And I promise not to go on about Natasha. I want to move on. What do you say?"

I wondered what 'moving on' might mean. The dinner almost sounded romantic; a double rebound bonanza. Not a good idea for either of us. In the end, I went with my gut instinct that Joseph wasn't as daft as that, or as rash as he seemed at that minute. Anyway, I could hold my own ground, I imagined.

"Okay, why not?"

We met up the following evening. His hotel was comfortable and the main dining room didn't disappoint, with windows overlooking the bay and lights twinkling from small boats chugging back to Elounda harbour. While we dined, he told me of his plans for the week and I was surprised to see he was bouncing back from his recent disappointment with more confidence than I'd have imagined. He said he was hiring a car the next day and planned to see a lot more of this part of Crete to make it a proper holiday.

"If you want to come along, you're very welcome, since you haven't got a car. And you seem to know more about the island than I do."

"Okay, I may do that. There's certainly more places here I'd like to see."

"We'll sort something out," he said with a fetching smile.

He handed me one of his business cards and scribbled his room number on the back and the phone number of the hotel. Then I heard a bit more about his disastrous love affair. It was me who teased it out. My interest was too piqued now not to. There wasn't much else in it though. He'd arrived in Edinburgh as a young manager of an upcoming chic hotel that had been looking for bright new talent. He knew no-one there, and even less about Scotland. He was lonely to start with and needed to establish a network. In his search for love he'd run headlong into a desperate relationship with Natasha, even though he knew she was married, and about to separate – or so she said. It was all a youthful error of judgement, as was coming to Greece for a meet-up where he knew no-one. '*Pathima, mathima*' as the Greeks say. Live and learn.

Our first outing together was to the Palace of Knossos and we rambled around the celebrated archaeological site. The next day Joseph was keen to go on a two-hour drive to the famous village of Matala on the south coast, with its iconic sandstone cliff-face pockmarked by natural caves said to have once been Roman grave sites. In the 1960s and 70s the area lured hippy dropouts and arty visitors who moved into the caves. However, most cave dwellers were driven out by the local authorities in the 1980s, so there was little to see now apart from a few shops and cafés, but the location was spectacular, overlooking the Libyan Sea. Joni Mitchell had famously visited and took up residence for a time in one of the caves, which inspired her hit song *Carey*.

"The wind is in from Africa
Last night I couldn't sleep"

Joseph seemed keen to find out which cave Mitchell had lived in, but it proved harder than expected, with various Greeks we asked claiming different caves as the sanctified abode.

"I suppose you know that Joni Mitchell was supposed to have come here to get over a broken relationship."

"I didn't know that," he said, turning towards me, his eyes wide with interest.

I'm sure he did but I dropped the subject. We walked down to the edge of the water and sat on the beach as the sun beat down on us mercilessly. With no wind, and the starkness of the cliff formation on the beach's northern flank, it suddenly felt like a sweltering August day. We got up and trailed through the shallow water, cooling off.

Joseph was happier that day than I'd ever seen him. At least he seemed to be getting over his disappointment with Natasha.

"Thanks for coming with me on these excursions. It's just what I needed," he said.

"Think nothing of it. I hate driving in Greece, so you've done *me* a favour. And it's been fun." And it had been. We'd got on better than I could have imagined and during a long lunch earlier in a beachside taverna we'd had plenty to talk about as usual.

"I wish I'd thought to bring my swimming costume," I said, gazing at the dazzling aquamarine water stretching out in front of us.

"You could always go in naked," he said, arching his brows at me.

I looked around the beach, with its scattering of back-packer tourists, and laughed. "Well, this is the place for it, isn't it? But I don't know if I'm daft enough for that. What about you?"

"Oh, you know me, the water's always too cold," he said, with a vibrant smirk.

We were up to our knees in water now. He was smiling, his tussled hair hanging over his forehead. I felt drawn to him and he leaned in towards me slowly. I knew we were about to kiss and the thought of it was unexpectedly appealing on that alluring shoreline. Just as our faces almost touched, I snapped out of the moment and turned away. *Get a grip*, I thought. I'd come to Crete partly to get over a relationship. He'd just been dumped by the married minx. How would that end? I felt hot and flustered and walked further into the sea until the water was well over the hem of my shorts. My God, it felt cool! What the hell! I dived straight into the water. It felt deliciously refreshing and sweet, like quenching a massive thirst.

I started swimming fast, as if I had it in my mind to swim to Africa, then I stopped, floating slowly about in the deep blue expanse of water. I could hear Joseph laughing from the shoreline, probably thinking I'd gone mad after all. It was the most memorable swim of my holiday and I was reluctant to leave the water, even when I'd had enough, because it's one thing to be daft and spontaneous but I'd have to pay for it by having to sit in the boiling sun while my soaked shorts and T-shirt dried, or return to Elounda sopping wet.

When I walked out of the water finally, he looked amused. "You are one crazy woman, but I kind of envied you. Was it nice?"

"It was gorgeous. You could have come in as well."

He cocked his head to the side and pressed his lips together in a gesture of regret, I thought, though regret for what exactly I couldn't be sure.

When we returned to the car, I was still dripping wet. Joseph had a towel in the boot so I took off my shorts and wrapped the towel around me so I wouldn't mess up the car seat. I remembered then we'd bought T-shirts earlier in a village shop. They had 'Matala, Crete' inscribed on them and a line drawing of caves underneath. A bit kitsch but useful now. I changed into it while Joseph waited in the car.

On the drive back to Elounda we didn't talk much. I felt sleepy after the swim. I was glad Joseph had the good sense earlier not to follow me into the sea. With or without his clothes it would have been the precursor to something more sensual, more risky. How appropriate though, in the surroundings. Wasn't that what Matala had always been about? Free love, free life. Cocking a snook at good sense? And then walking away, no regrets, no complications. If only passion could always be that easy to engage with.

Over the next few days, we continued our tours around eastern Crete, without a repeat of the near-kiss at the beach, though there were times when we were almost there. Subliminally, we both knew it would have been a bad idea. But our days together were happy and Joseph was good company and much more upbeat, as if sloughing off his mucky affair with Natasha had liberated him somewhat. I noticed during our time together that he was developing huge enthusiasm for Greece and talked a lot about it, asking many questions. It was now his favourite holiday destination, he said, so all had not been lost for him coming here. And in the end, I was sorry to see him go.

On the day Joseph left, I waited with him in the *plateia* in Elounda for the bus to Herakleion. When we heard it in the distance, he fumbled in his shoulder bag for something, his wavy hair flopping over his eyes. He looked vulnerable and sweet. He took out yet another business card and wrote a phone number on the back.

"It's my home number too. If you feel like extending your holiday after Thessaloniki and coming to Scotland, give me a call. Maybe a trip back to the homeland would be a nice conclusion to your sabbatical," he said, squeezing my arm gently.

I put the card in my pocket. "Thanks, Joseph, but I don't think I can make it to Scotland on this trip. My boss in Sydney wouldn't appreciate it, I'm sure. But I'll be back in Blighty before too long."

"Sure, any time, though I don't know how long I'll be there myself."

I gave him a quizzical look.

"I'm formulating a plan, you see. I feel like a complete change now after what's happened recently. I like the idea of coming back here to Crete to work in a hotel. I think it might be fab and our sightseeing trip here has really fired up the idea."

I was stunned. "I wouldn't do anything rash. Give it a year or so."

"I will, don't worry. Greece is really coming on, isn't it? I'm thinking of all the hotels they've got planned for the bay here. I've been checking it out. This could be a new luxury destination for Greece."

He'd been right on the money with that because years later the strip of luxury hotels along the bay, some of which were still on the drawing board, would turn the area into one of the chicest tourist spots in Greece.

"So, maybe we could meet here instead."

"You're making a habit now of Elounda meet-ups, Joseph," I said with a teasing smile.

He laughed, but the irony wasn't lost on him.

"Thanks again for listening to my troubles. In the end it's been a terrific holiday – mainly thanks to you."

He blushed and reached forward to give me a powerful hug. I felt a strong, silly urge to say I'd extend my holiday after all and come to Scotland. The words were hovering on my lips and then he kissed me, holding it for a moment. He turned away just as we heard the bus approaching, clattering fully laden towards the bus stop. While we watched passengers alighting, another thought started yammering in my head: what if I asked him to stay a bit longer in Elounda, what if, what if!

Too late! He picked up his travel bag. "Keep in touch. I'd love to know how your trip north goes."

"Yes, I certainly will," I said, sounding more chipper than I felt.

People were boarding and Joseph stepped on to the bus quickly and took his seat. I waited while everyone else clambered aboard. I watched the bus turn out of the *plateia* and rumble into the distance, a cloud of dust in its slipstream.

I felt slightly lost in the days after Joseph left, which I hadn't expected. I kept going over my short attachment to him, wondering if it might have ended differently, or should have. But after a while I let it go, turning my attention to the imminent trip north. Soon enough I was saying goodbye to Polina and Kostas. They had been among the kindest Greeks I'd ever met. I felt like I was saying goodbye to part of my own family, even though I was certain I probably wouldn't see them again, or at least not for a long time. I'd always think of them, particularly our fishing trip and that glorious sunrise over Mirabello Bay.

Some friendships that are sparked on long holidays survive over the years, but mostly they don't because they are the product of the place they were sired in and often that's where the commonality ends, sadly. I suspected that might be the same with Joseph if I took him up one day on his Scottish offer. There had been an attraction between us – not something we spoke about, but there all the same, deliciously untouched. Yet for all his sweetness and charm, his affair with Natasha showed he was still very much a rookie at falling in love. But aren't we all?

I returned to Athens healthier and happier and started to think about the event I'd been sent to Greece for in the first place, the international Tourism Expo in Thessaloniki. It was no easy matter, as my head was full of fishing, *horta*, Greek soaps, leper colonies, love affairs crashing, and one still festering sweetly at the back of my mind. I sensed I looked a bit rough-edged and rural by the time I found the city office of the PR company organising the travel trip for the group of journalists, all Australian, bound for the northern city. When I saw the planned itinerary for the week ahead, I was shocked to see it had glam events like the cocktail party on the old sailing ship in Thessaloniki's harbour with the mayor, which I would otherwise have loved, but now I felt anxious. I had nothing glam to wear, having spent weeks in rural bliss, happier to amble about in sandals and shorts rather than smart outfits. My best outfit, a black sleeveless dress, was nowhere near smart enough, and too summery. I would need to go shopping – in a hurry.

With a couple of days to spare in Athens I visited shopping areas I remembered from previous trips, such as Kolonaki. The area was a cool expanse of cafés, bookshops and fashionable clothing shops that I could never have afforded when I was teaching English and looking after kids in the 1970s. I managed a haircut, a few decent outfits for evening, shoes and a smart woollen coat, as I was told Thessaloniki was cold in mid-November. I had little room for all this in my overstuffed suitcase, which meant I had to leave some of my Cretan casuals behind at the hotel, though not my Matala T-shirt. That would stay with me for years.

The visit to Thessaloniki was the expected media whirlwind of city bus tours, museums, restaurants and the Expo itself, which was unintentionally amusing, particularly the conference sessions in Greek for visitors and delegates, with simultaneous translation via headphones. One topic I remember well was the vexed issue of making Greek cities clean and inviting for foreign visitors, a perennial topic in Greek life, which goes on even today. One of the local Greek speakers, who seemed to have gate-crashed the podium and was probably a disgruntled environmentalist or a poorly paid government worker, yammered on in fast Greek about how cities, including this one, were unfit for visitors: rubbish bins overflowing with garbage, streets rife with stray cats and dogs and so forth. Even the translator lost her thread at one point and struggled to keep up with the interloper, which caused ripples of laughter throughout the auditorium, with an official scrambled to the stage to heave the poor guy away. It was the highlight of the morning and made me realise, not for the first time, that Greeks always play by their own rules wherever possible, a position that finally got them into trouble in the economic crisis in 2010 after having messed up their fiscal spreadsheets for decades.

Thessaloniki is a fascinating city, with an exotic mix of Greek and Levantine culture, and before World War Two was one of the most cosmopolitan cities in the Mediterranean, with an integrated population of Greeks, Turks and Jews, though tragically most of the Jewish population was wiped out when the Germans occupied the city during the war and sent them to concentration camps. The city has a wealth of archaeology and history and stretches from the hills down to a long shoreline on the Thermaic Gulf, bordered by a line of apartment buildings and the famous 15th century White Tower. The city has been occupied by the Romans, Byzantines, Ottomans – and latterly by garrulous Aussie journalists.

The Expo trip had been better than expected, if hectic, and the only low point was my slip-up with a canape on the mayor's boat trip. What I thought was salmon bedded down in puff pastry turned out to be a devilish prawn, hence my quick dash downstairs to part with it, in case I became victim to another bout of enteritis, necessitating another month in Crete perhaps! Or Scotland?

At the end of the week, the journalists had one free afternoon to themselves and while some decided to trail about the bars and cool coffee shops of the city, raising hell, I chose to tramp about the city with a map in hand but no real plans. Just before sunset I found myself near the waterfront on a narrow street, the sea glimmering ahead of me. I was desperate to sit down and have a rest. There was a café on the corner with a few chairs and tables outside and as I came level with them, a lone, older woman, smoking and drinking Greek coffee, looked up and said something in Greek I didn't catch, and then in English. "You're the angel I've been waiting for today. Come sit with me a moment." She pulled out the chair beside her and tapped its rattan seat.

I was in no mood for a stranger making fey pronouncements. Or perhaps I was more tired than I thought and I felt like no kind of angel. I wondered if it might be easier to just smile and walk on to another café. But I didn't. She looked a bit intriguing, bohemian you might say, with a bright embroidered kind of coat, her dyed brown hair piled up on her head in a messy up-do. She might have been an ageing opera singer or an artist. Or no-one at all.

I sat beside her. She stubbed out her cigarette and drained the last of her coffee. She ordered a carafe of red wine. It came with two glasses.

"You will have a glass, yes?

"Yes, okay, thanks."

"My name is Nefeli, by the way, and yours?"

I told her mine. She preferred to call me Margarita, like most Greeks always do.

"Nefeli is ancient in origin, if it interests you. It means cloudy. Zeus created her from clouds and she was also the mother of the mythical Centaurs."

"It's a lovely name. I like it."

"I like it too, and it suits me, I think. People often say I look rather sad, but I prefer to think I'm just overcast at times," she said, with a mock frown.

Her English was good and as we sipped our wine she wanted to know where I was from and what I was doing in Thessaloniki so late in the year. I gave her a quick outline of my Expo week, leaving out the earlier part of my sabbatical. I told her about the tours, the Expo conference, the stroppy environmentalist, the harbour cruise, drunken Aussie journalists for company, making the most of their media freebie.

"You have seen more of the city than most then. And by the way, the environmentalist was quite right about the state of our streets sometimes. I wish I'd been there. What fun!" she laughed, a throaty smoker's laugh, and it scattered a few of her clouds away briefly.

Nefeli was a beautiful older woman with a dignified, interesting face and big, dark eyes that glimmered the way old mirrors do in candlelight. I could tell she'd had a fascinating life. But incredibly she was one of the rarest people I'd ever met, who didn't want to talk about herself at all. She waved her hand in the air when I asked her.

"Oh, my dear, you don't want to hear my story. We would be here for weeks. It would, as I think you English say, make your ears bleed," she said, taking a big mouthful of wine. "What I can say is that I am Jewish and I'm still here in this city, a big achievement if you know anything about our history. But if you are here for much longer, or you come back some day, call by and see me, my dear, and I'll tell you all about it. As a journalist, it may interest you. At the café, everyone knows me and where I live."

I felt unexpectedly sad that I was flying back to Sydney the next day, for all kinds of reasons, and it would have been interesting to talk more with Nefeli. I took her address anyway and I promised to write. I don't know why. I hardly knew her at all. We talked a while about different things, mostly impersonal matters, and then I said I had to leave. She squeezed my hand tight and kissed me on the cheek.

"Tell me one thing, Nefeli, before I go. Why did you say earlier I was the angel you'd been waiting for? What did you mean by that?"

She closed her eyes a moment and smiled. "Ah … I saw you in the distance. You looked friendly. *Filiki.* Someone nice to share a glass of wine with, which you have been, my friend. Sometimes in this life that's all you want at the end of the day. A sympathetic friend and someone with a different story. I like that. It makes me forget my own for a while."

As I walked away, the melancholy of Nefeli's last words made my eyes prickle with tears. It didn't take me long to reach the top of the street and I turned around to give her a final wave, but she was gone. If it hadn't been for the empty carafe and wine glasses I might have thought she'd never been there, and that I'd imagined her. Or had Nefeli simply dissipated like a whirl of gossamer clouds, taken back by Zeus on some other mission? I smiled to myself. Whether or not she was real, Nefeli was intriguing, someone I would never have met so easily, so spontaneously, anywhere else but Greece. And that applied also to Joseph, and Polina and Kostas, so easily met, so indelibly etched in my imagination. It was a delicious thought to end my Greek sabbatical – and to plan the next one.

12

Myths and mayhem

THERE are few things more nerve-racking than arriving at a foreign destination late at night, one that's completely new to you that you'll shortly have to navigate in a hire car. Jim and I landed at Volos airport, in the Pelion region of Greece, one hot August night. Half an hour later, at 10.30pm, we were still there, waiting outside at a metal coffee table to see the young hire car guy. There was a small queue in the coffee shop – his 'office'. It all seemed to take ages, but the guy was genial and after all the paperwork was signed, he explained how to get to Volos city, 12 miles away at the head of the Pagasitikos Gulf.

We had booked a room for the night at the Volos Palace Hotel, with the intention of an early start next day, driving to a rental holiday house in the south of the long Pelion peninsula, which extends from its northerly mountain range to a narrow slip of land at the bottom. It has the gulf on one side and the wilder Aegean Sea on the other.

We had brought our sat-nav unit because we planned to do a lot of driving around Pelion. The hire car guy blithely waved us off, saying the drive to the city would be easy. "Just follow the signs to Volos," he said. And we headed off towards the bright city lights in the distance, nestling in front of the western flank of the mountains.

So what could possibly go wrong? Well, everything really. This was Greece, after all, a country that we knew, after years living in the southern mainland, could spin you a curved ball at any time. The drive started off fine, until we reached the motorway exit for Volos. It was closed for road repairs. Why hadn't the hire car guy mentioned this? Who knows?

We were forced to keep heading north on the motorway, which was not where we wanted to go. A few diversion signs on the way weren't helpful, as Volos didn't seem to figure on any of them. On we went, becoming more and more anxious and lost, the dippy sat-nav announcer woman yammering out unfathomable requests as the night was slipping by. Luckily, we did find a place to do U-turn in the end, and headed south again.

Again it was sheer luck we spotted an exit slip-road marked Volos. Jim punched the air with relief as we drove towards the western edge of the city. But when we got there, we faced even bigger problems. Every road into the city seemed to be having road repairs as well, with closures and yet more diversion signs and traffic cones. Why would the city fathers want to do this in August, the busiest month in Greece? And so began a tormenting, rubber-burning foray into the city and out again (so many times we lost count) desperately searching for the road (any road!) that would lead us to the hotel near the port area. There was no point in stopping pedestrians because I've found the Greeks (God bless them!) are like the Irish, with directions that are generally colourful but illogical and always get you into more strife.

We could actually see the neon sign on the Volos Palace Hotel twinkling in the distance, but we could never quite reach it because of the roadworks, and we had to concentrate more on Greek drivers (equally frazzled) pulling maverick stunts, especially on roundabouts. It was now nearly midnight. We were exhausted and hungry, and Jim resorted to a few strops (unusually for him) at the wheel. The sat-nav woman had also gone off her trolley, a gibbering wreck by now, spitting out instructions that she instantly cancelled and updated seconds later, and all in her crazy, mispronounced Greek.

At one point she pleaded pointlessly for us to try for the 'Lambro Gorilla'. We laughed every time she said it.

"What's that, do you think? A Latin American dance move, or a strong cocktail," I quizzed Jim.

"I'd kill for a Lambro cocktail, no worries about that," he replied, wiping a sheen of sweat off his forehead.

We parked for a minute in a side street to gather our thoughts. Jim looked beyond tired with a haunted, harassed look in his eyes. We were close to giving up, dumping the car near the hotel, and lugging our suitcases there on foot, when a young couple swung by. I wound down the window and was forced to plead for their help as the sat-nav woman gabbled on. The Greek girl pointed at the dashboard.

"Forget the crap sat-nav. It never works for Volos." Or words to that effect. What did work for Volos? I wondered. But I shut if off anyway. It was high time.

"You are so close to the hotel anyway," the girl said, offering directions. In true Greek style, the route she recommended sounded irrational. In the end we winged it and got to the hotel after about 10 minutes, even snagging a parking space outside.

The four-star Volos Palace looked plush on the outside but inside it seemed like a relic from another era (well before Greece's economic crisis) with plenty of marble and swish curtains, but it seemed tired, like the guy on reception. We were at our wit's end now and starving. We asked about room service and were told emphatically 'no'. "All the catering staff have gone home now." What in August? Twelve-thirty in Greece, in August, is just about the right time to head out to dinner with the whole family in tow. This wasn't a sleepy night in the Cotswolds! There seemed to be no-one in the hotel, apart from a few residents hugging the bar, watching football on TV. We were given a city map, however, and shown where we could find a 'lively' street with a huddle of tavernas.

On the map it seemed easy to get there but in reality, it wasn't (of course not!). It was a longish walk beside a wide busy road, not blocked anywhere, miraculously, and as we trudged along we discovered finally what a Lambro Gorilla was. It's a major road to the harbour area called Grigoriou Lambraki, named after a 1960s' Greek hero, which the sat-nav minx had mashed up horribly. We had a good laugh at that, wondering why the hell we bothered with sat-nav and all that flaky Euro blah-blah. It wasn't the first time we'd had a total mess-up with the same sat-nav minx. While driving years ago to Koroni in Messinia for the first time, she kept warning us about 'Calamitous Coronaries' on the road that was signposted Kalamata to Koroni. Time for a new sat-nav system.

We were almost ready to give up when we finally saw signs of life: a street with a *kafeneio* and a souvlaki joint still buzzing, which is usual on hot summer nights in Greek cities. It had a nice vibe, with a few tables and chairs on the pavement, people sitting about eating and drinking. This was more like it. The staff were helpful, bringing us not only two servings of souvlaki wrapped in warm pita bread but also little bowls of salads and Pelion specialties, which we hadn't ordered. And a couple of cold Mythos beers. For the first time since we'd arrived hours earlier, we felt our shoulders drop with relief, and we tucked in.

We mentioned the road block disaster to the owner. He grimaced and waved one arm around in the diverting fashion of Greeks when they're hacked off. "No-one knows why the council does things this way. Ridiculous!" he complained. Just another imponderable to add to the load of crisis anxieties this country has faced for years. But despite everything, it's the conviviality of Greeks that makes you love this country and keeps you coming back.

The next morning, after a hearty hotel breakfast (the staff had returned), we'd recovered from our arrival anxieties. But I can't say we felt rested because all night long from our front room we could hear people trudging up and down the street below, going home in the early hours, doing all the things I expected in August, of course, but didn't think would happen right beside our bedroom window, full volume. Old guys were half stewed and singing Greek songs, some were loudly shouting '*Chronia Polla*!' (a common Greek wish, 'many years' for birthdays etc) and one group seemingly arguing endlessly. Greeks often sound like they're arguing, even when discussing trifling issues like the price of tomato yields.

However, the drive south from Volos was a dream. The views of the long gulf reminded us strongly of the Messinian Gulf, with Kalamata at its head, with a series of small coves along the coast, some quite remote. The other side of the peninsula faces the Aegean Sea, close to the islands of Skiathos and Skopelos. Some of the beaches on the Aegean side, especially in the north, are stunning, like Papa Nero and Damouchari, where some of the beach scenes in the first *Mamma Mia!* movie were filmed.

It's a unique region dominated by the Pelion mountainous in the north, fabled in ancient times as the home of the legendary centaurs (half man/half horse) and called the 'Mountain of the Centaurs'. Volos city is believed to have been inhabited since 700 BC. There have been Neolithic and Mycenaean settlements here and a trip to Volos's Athanassakeio Archeological Museum is a must, with its small but perfect collection of antiquities.

We had booked a villa for a month near the small southern town of Argalasti, close to the gulf side. One morning, while enjoying a coffee in the town's *plateia,* we spotted a dishevelled English-looking guy, with unkempt white hair, dressed in an old T-shirt and baggy shorts, ambling along the pavement nearby and swinging a couple of plastic bags bulging with groceries.

"Hey, that bloke looks like Stanley Johnson – father of Boris," said Jim. It certainly was him, and we'd previously read how Stanley owned a plush holiday villa near Argalasti, where his Prime Minister son often stayed. "Shall we go over and tell him we think Boris is a buffoon and Brexit is rubbish?" We didn't, but we had a good laugh over the sighting.

We spent the first week or two exploring beaches while the weather was hot and the sea was calm, and there are some remote locations here that don't disappoint, such as Ayia Kyriaki, an old-style fishing settlement with a backdrop of the Tiseo Mountains, and Tzasteni, an impossibly picturesque cove encircled on one side by small white houses. But we had planned mostly to make several excursions into the Pelion mountains because it's this area that makes the region so unique, with villages like Makrinitsa, Milies and Tzagarada, which to my mind are like the villages I remember from my very early trips to Greece.

Makrinitsa is an enchanting place with a huge, elegant *plateia*, shaded by tall plane trees, and with a dizzying view over Volos city. Classed as an area of 'cultural interest', and therefore protected from modern development, it has probably changed little over the centuries and owes much to its wealthy trading past, with grand buildings in classic Pelion style: a mix of local stone at the bottom and mud-bricked, whitewashed upper floors with wide wooden eaves.

Off the square there's a narrow cobbled pathway with one of the village's most famous hangouts, the Café Ouzeri Theophilos, named after the famous folk artist Theofilos Hatzimihail, who frequented this place and painted a fresco over one wall with the theme of the 1821 Greek War of Independence which is still intact. You really do feel the weight of Greek history and culture in this village. And the Art and History Museum of Pelion can't be missed, though it probably often is, as it's down a cobbled (*kalderimi*) stone path, which is not easy to locate. However, situated in the old Topali mansion, which belonged to a former wealthy merchant and built in 1844, it's a unique window into the region's history and has now been taken over by the Ministry of Culture.

The museum was just about to shut when we got there but the young Greek guide was generous in keeping it open a while longer and gave us a tour. He was particularly knowledgeable about the village's own 1878 revolution against the Ottoman Turks and there are interesting artefacts here, including a framed picture of the British correspondent for *The Times* newspaper, Charles Ogle. In his twenties, he went to Pelion to report on the battle with the Turks. While helping Makrinitsa to repel the Turks after a massacre of the villagers, he was murdered by members of the Turkish army. While hardly known in Britain, he's a Pelion hero on a par with Lord Byron, and the city of Volos has a street named after him.

Tsagarada is a smaller village on a steep mountain slope and slightly off the beaten track and accessed by a long road, with challenging zigzags. The setting and especially the old *plateia* is classy, in the shade of a famous 1,000-year-old plane tree. It has an otherworldly feel to it as well. On the side of the church in the *plateia* was a glass case with curious old pictures of local weddings, groups of villagers like Victorians in severe, long outfits, with a ghostly pallor to their faces, probably from the pictures being old and kept outside for so long. The village is also swaddled by verdant slopes, which were misty even on a hot day, and a perfect location for some bolshy centaurs to run amok.

But we were about to see something much scarier. We had walked down from the *plateia* to a small park to have our takeaway cold drinks and were so engrossed in the view down the valley towards the Aegean side of the peninsula we didn't take too much notice of our immediate surroundings.

"Do you hear a strange noise?" I asked Jim. "A kind of thrumming noise."

"Maybe this mountainside always thrums – with mythical beings," said Jim wistfully, sucking on his lemonade.

But after a while it annoyed me, so I got up and walked towards a row of trees behind us. I froze.

"Critter alarm!" I called loudly.

During our four years in Greece, we had frequently been visited by unwanted critters: snakes, scorpions, mutant caterpillars, moany expats! We had an aversion to anything with tails, stingers and noise. The call was our agreed signal when anything threatening marched into view.

"Holy shit!" said Jim when he came over to see what I was festering about.

We stood and stared a moment at the biggest hornets' nest we'd ever seen, on the trunk of a tree, with hundreds of them, the big brown and red variety with long dangly legs like F-111s, which we'd only ever seen one at a time, not in a whole squadron.

We grabbed our bags and fled like the wind back up the slope to the village and didn't look back or stop until we reached the *plateia*. Even then I had horrible visions of the hornets chasing us up the slope in an angry, thrumming ribbon of flight.

The mountain area may be famous for its mythological creatures but why don't people ever tell you about the hornets?

13

May contain dogs

WHEN we formulated our plan for a Greek adventure, just as the economic crisis was unfolding, we revealed some of its early details to a rather sardonic Scottish neighbour. We told him we would be taking Wallace, our much-loved Jack Russell terrier. He looked horrified.

"You're not taking Wallace to Greece? Haven't they got enough problems there already?"

We laughed because he was quite right. Probably Greece in a crisis wasn't ready for a hyperactive dog like Wallace, with a big, joyful personality but a stubborn, maverick soul. Like many terriers, he had been difficult to train, even though there had been compelling reasons why we hadn't been able to put as much time into it as we would have liked, which I detailed in my first memoir, *Things Can Only Get Feta*. What he had probably needed when we bought him as a puppy, just a year after we moved to Scotland, was a dog whisperer like the well-known American TV celebrity, Cesar Millan.

One of the main issues with Wallace was that he regularly ignored commands when outside, not uncommon with Jack Russells, especially those in pursuit of real or imagined rabbits. There were some memorable occasions when Wallace was off the lead, out in the Scottish fields, and the only word that would bring him back was '*chicken*!' (his favourite food). And there was one instance in our hillside village in Greece when Wallace slipped out of the house and infiltrated a religious procession, with chaotic results. With us in hot pursuit, the '*chicken!*' word had to be mobilised, with the volume ramped up, much to the surprise and censure of the villagers. In a location with several tavernas, they knew exactly what this English word meant and it had no place in a sombre religious event.

I had highlighted this incident in *Things Can Only Get Feta,* and after the book was published in America, I was amused to be told by a fellow writer in Chicago that she had read passages of the book to her young daughter. Maria's little girl went through a comical phase of calling out 'chicken!' to every small terrier dog she saw in the street, thinking this was the best way to get their attention.

There were times in Wallace's early years when I had to phone his Edinburgh breeder, Brigit, for some guidance on his fizzy, eccentric behaviour. She had bred Jack Russells for decades and had shown many of her pedigree terriers at the famous Crufts dog show. Wallace wasn't Crufts material (why put chaos in an enclosed space?) but he was a pedigree, registered with the British Kennel Club and carried an unintentionally snooty title along with it: 'Wallace of Wyn-tersted', named after the old Victorian house we'd bought in Scotland, Wallace's first real home.

When I explained some of Wallace's issues to Brigit, she replied, "Och, dear. All my dogs have the naughty gene, I'm afraid." I was stunned. Brigit had a heart of gold but why hadn't she imparted this wisdom when we'd bought Wallace? Or had we just been in denial about her wayward terriers?

From our first visit to Brigit's farmhouse to see Wallace, it was obvious really how eccentric most of her older dogs were, dragging their dried pigs' ears (dog treats) round the kitchen, or leaping on to your lap to lick your ears. But they were endearing beasts, all toffs and all related to Wallace, like his cousin Dumpy (the ear licker), his uncle Archie, his grandmother Tallulah. What's not to like? But I quickly realised that Wallace would probably never change – and why should he? As Brigit often said, "He's a Jack Russell, dear, not a poodle!" True enough. This is a clever breed of dog with a mind like a steel trap but with a massive dollop of individuality and spontaneity. You had to take the whole mix. Simple as that.

From his early years, Wallace barked a lot at strangers and although I understood why he did it, and there isn't scope here to explain all the reasons, let's just say he saw most people in our Scottish village as pesky, interfering folk – and sometimes he was right. Often the people Wallace barked at were those I wasn't sure about myself. And I discovered early on too that people have a sense of entitlement with other people's puppies. They see one and make a grab for it, to pick it up, hold it. Not all dogs are okay with that, just as children aren't. Wallace didn't go for huggy behaviour and let the offenders know with a lusty round of barking. When we were out with Wallace in the village, he used to bark loudly when he spotted one particular old guy we knew, who in response would flatten himself comically against walls and fences, with outstretched arms, and groan in mock horror. It always raised a laugh, but deep down Wallace probably terrified him – or the other way round. I have to say the old guy scared the bejesus out of me at times.

So taking a dog to a country that doesn't put pets on pedestals was always going to be a challenge, especially a rural area where dogs are generally working creatures, chained up in fields. On a purely practical level, taking Wallace also meant several vet's appointments for microchipping, pet passport, drug treatments for tropical infestations and diseases and so forth. Most dogs are creatures of habit and don't always react well to upheavals in their lives. I had wondered how Wallace would deal with ferries, stranger danger, ship's horns, loud-speakers and long car journeys through Europe without having meltdowns. I even asked our Scottish vet to prescribe some mild canine tranquillisers to help ease Wallace through the journey. They didn't work but in the end it didn't matter because Wallace rose to the occasion; he handled everything brilliantly, and only went bonkers a couple of times with people who were, frankly, odder than he was.

At a service station in Switzerland, I sat in the car with Wallace while Jim paid for the petrol. A couple of dishevelled hitchhikers drew up beside my open window and asked if they could get a ride with us for a few kilometres. I laughed out loud and pointed towards the back seat, loaded up with suitcases and bags, and Wallace sandwiched into one corner in his dog bed.

"No room, obviously," I said. They frowned and hung about anyway, peering annoyingly through the back windows. I started feeling nervous, wondering if they were about to carjack us, and Jim was still in the petrol station. But Wallace had finally had enough of the pesky pair and started up the characteristic slightly screamy barking he adopted when he was feeling threatened, after which the pair turned and shuffled off to another car waiting behind.

"Good work, Wallace. I didn't like them either," I said, pleased at his intuition.

While I understood most of Wallace's crazy turns, sometimes his outbursts were incredibly badly timed. In Italy, we checked into a large hotel (part of a chain) that claimed to be dog friendly. Wallace was fine at reception and sat quietly while we dealt with formalities. Then two teenagers walked past on their way out, talking loudly in Italian, waving their arms about, and Wallace started a bit of screamy barking. The guy at reception pulled a massive face.

"I hope he don't bark like that in your room. We cannot allow that," he grizzled. That made Wallace worse. We all got properly told off then.

"You take the dog out of the hotel tonight for dinner tonight. You don't leave him alone in the room, shouting every five minutes, upsetting guests," said Little Mussolini.

Not shouting as much as you, I thought, but to head off any more problems Jim bundled Wallace under his arm and we dragged our cases to the lift. I was reminded then of Cornish chef Rick Stein, who once had a comical JR called Chalky, who famously starred in his early TV foodie/travel programmes. Stein lamented in one programme that when he was away filming and took Chalky he often had to smuggle the dog into hotel rooms in bags and baskets to keep him out of sight because he had a habit of trying to nip strangers if they got too familiar. I know how he felt.

"What was all that about at reception, with Wallace and Signor Snippy?" said Jim, as we finally got to our room.

I shrugged. "Who knows? The sound of Italian possibly? But you know Wallace. Sometimes there are people he just doesn't like."

When Wallace was young we realised he didn't like a lot of noise, including people shouting and screaming, crockery rattling, vacuum cleaners thrumming, bees buzzing, horns blaring, that sort of thing. But there was something else. I'd discovered over the years Wallace was really quite conventional and prissy for a Jack Russell. He didn't like folk wearing outlandish clothes: funny hats, eye-watering colours and so forth. I was sure that one of the reasons he'd had a strop in the hotel foyer was because he didn't like the receptionist's diverting outfit: apple green trousers; green loafers, a bright blueberry-coloured jacket. I didn't much care for the colour clash myself. It was hellish! So Wallace was also something of a fashionista as well. Who knew?

When we got to Greece we knew that having an active dog like Wallace was always going to limit where we could stay, and a few of the decent rental properties we looked at (as opposed to the dismal dumps with scant furniture, damp walls, wires hanging out of walls) were not fenced properly and a 'jumper' like Wallace would easily escape. Many owners simply didn't want a dog on their property.

We picked the house in Megali Mantineia because it was secure, with a stone wall, and quiet, not overlooked by other houses. The owner was happy to have a dog there.

"Are you choosing this house just for Wallace?" the estate agent laughingly asked us. And in a way we had to, otherwise nothing would quite work out. But here's the thing: all the choices we made to help Wallace turned out to be great choices in general. He led us unintentionally to the best location for this adventure and to the best side of Greek life, or rather to the authentic side we'd been searching for. Having him with us also created talking points with Greeks and created many friendships.

We took him with us many times when we visited Foteini at her *ktima*. She wasn't a dog person, or a cat person really. Her passion was goats. She could hug a goat until its eyes watered but was wary of Wallace near her personal space. One day he came with us for one of our regular 'coffee mornings' with her. There was the usual amount of rubbish around her café spot (a ramshackle place on the farm with a shoogly plastic table and scuffed chairs under a hornet-strafed fruit tree). I put Wallace up on one of the chairs to spare him from fallen mulberries and critters. He sat quietly and yet Foteini pulled a face like curdled milk.

"You let the dog sit on chairs?" she said, her hands sternly on her hips. I laughed. The chair had five coats of grime and wobbly legs. Wallace was cleaner.

However, none of it really surprised us. We'd been slightly prepared for negativity about having a dog in Greece because of other trips we'd made. We'd seen a lot of feral and abandoned dogs trying to bump along with locals, mainly with poor outcomes.

On a trip to Corfu, before our odyssey in the southern mainland, we were staying on the soporific north-east coast, often described as Kensington-on-sea because of its colony of well-heeled expats, including millionaire bankers. We had rented a smart villa with a swimming pool and were looking forward to a serene two weeks. On the first morning we opened the French windows of our top-floor bedroom and gazed down from the balcony to see a big sandy-coloured dog, of indeterminate provenance, stretched out on a sunbed by the pool.

"What the hell!" said Jim as we watched the dog lying on his back, enjoying the morning sunshine. We dressed and wandered down to check out the interloper and found he wasn't aggressive and quite biddable. He was hungry and with dismay we noticed he had a least one fat tick on his eyebrow. And he was probably full of other critters. He had collar but it was old and faded, with no name tag. We fed him and then tried to shoo him out the front gate, but he wouldn't go. Anyway, there were so many holes in the boundary fences that it would have made no difference. He just sloped off back to his sunbed with a proprietorial sneer. It was comical in its way and we felt sorry for him, though the cleaning woman, who came every other day, didn't. We asked her how we should deal with the situation. She pulled a massive face.

"I don't know. He's been here for a few months now. I think he belonged to an English woman who had to return home and she left him behind. It is a shame but the owners of the villa don't really want him around," she said.

We didn't mention the dog again. We assumed if we complained too much the dog would be dealt harshly with, and it seemed luck had been on his side to have survived as long as he had – living his sunbed life. As salubrious as the north-east was, no-one seemed to have a plan for dealing with stray dogs or providing animal shelters, which is still the case in much of Greece. But day after day the dog was there. We kept feeding him but made sure he never sneaked inside the house.

One morning early in our stay we drove off to the beach after breakfast.

"You'll never guess what I can see in the rear-vision mirror," said Jim, moments after we'd turned from the driveway onto the coastal road. I looked out the back window and there was the dog, running after the car along the road like a favourite in the Grand National, cars behind honking at us. Jim put his foot on the gas – and so did the dog.

"He's still there!" said Jim, peering in the mirror. But after a while the poor skinny mutt gave up and sloped off home. It wasn't the only time he gave chase and often we had to distract him by waiting until we were ready to leave to dish out his food.

On the morning we were returning to the UK we felt despondent for poor old Road Runner, wondering how his future would pan out, so we gave him a heaped bowl of dog food. When we put the suitcases in the car, ready to leave, he looked sad, his head hanging low. I knew he'd obviously seen this routine countless times before, including the day his owner had sloped back to England. Despite leaving some tins of dog food in the kitchen and penning a pleading note for the cleaning woman, asking her to help find the dog some kind of home, I feared these days would probably be his last. And he knew it too. As we drove away, he never tried to follow us. I saw him turn slowly towards the pool, to the sun lounger no doubt, to enjoy whatever days of sunshine he had left.

We discovered during our four years in rural Greece that there were hazards galore for the dogs that foreigners brought to Greece: aggressive, unchained Greek hunting dogs in fields, which occasionally broke loose and gave chase; wild boars on wooded slopes, and snakes, and the problem of the *foles*, poisoned meat left out to kill foxes mainly, but which was often devoured by dogs off leads. We knew several expats who had lost pets this way. We rarely let Wallace off his lead for this reason alone but luckily he was too prissy about food. No rancid meat offerings for him.

For his part, Wallace walked lightly across the Greek landscape. No other dog, scabrous cat, goat or scorpion was ever harmed by him in the course of our odyssey. But it was a shame about the ancestral rug he ruined in the rented house in Monemvasia – and the less said about that the better. For all his mischief and ramped-up temperament, Wallace was an inimitable companion: tireless, fearless, a delightful dog who threw himself at life like a demolition ball. He leapt and bounded his way through the adventure, as if in joyful celebration of his own life. Wallace surpassed all expectations.

I often think of our Scottish friend's lament: "You're not taking Wallace to Greece?" And the simple truth is our long odyssey wouldn't have been quite the same without him, not as funny or dramatic. And in many ways, he even steered our destiny. Were it not for Wallace on the village road when we first arrived in Megali Mantineia, we would never have met Foteini, or not so easily perhaps because she stopped to ask us why we were taking a sheep for a walk, which is what Wallace resembled to Greeks who'd never seen a black-faced Jack Russell before. We would probably not have taken the dog-friendly stone house in this authentic hill village, a fact that set our odyssey on a particular course. It makes me think that dogs see a lot further along the road than we can, beyond the mythic rabbits, the chickens, the loud Italians in clashing colours. And no-one should ever doubt it!

14

How things Pan out in Arcadia

ARCADIA seems like the twin brother to Pelion, a place of myths and magic. The word alone conjures up images of pastoral bliss, amiable shepherds and the goat-legged god Pan twirling about the forests, playing his pipes, scaring the bejesus out of passing nymphs. It was an idealised place that inspired great writers, such as the poet Virgil, Shakespeare and a slew of European painters of the 18th and 19th centuries.

The appeal of Arcadia harks back to its ancient rural past, to an alluring simple lifestyle, but in reality the region would have also been rough about the edges, which more discerning, sniffy ancients would have described as Hicksville. These Arcadians would have been the butt of jokes, the way the Irish and the Cornish were in Britain not that long ago, and mockingly called 'hayseeds'. The ancient Oracle of Delphi was said to have referred to Arcadians, in a similar vein, as 'acorn-eaters'.

Arcadia is certainly very old. The Cadogan guidebook to the region, *Peloponnese and Athens,* describes it as "one of the best-kept secrets of the Peloponnese ... a place that seemed ancient even in ancient times". It has some Olympian provenance. Its founding father, Pelasgos, had a daughter, Kallisto, who was impregnated by Zeus. The various sons of Pelasgos, such as Mantineos, lent their name to some surviving regional cities. Plenty of major characters in the rural mix here.

We went one late summer to the Gortynia area of Arcadia, which is flush with mountains, rivers, gorges and remote natural retreats, and cooler than the surrounding plains, ideal for hiking about. Gortynia was historically an ideal hangout for resistance fighters against the Ottoman Turks, such as the great Theodoros Kolokotronis, hero of the Greek War of Independence in the 1820s. There is a cluster of unique villages here: Dimitsana, Karitaina and Zatouna, but we spent a few hours at the mountain eyrie of Stemnitsa, lauded as one of the 15 most beautiful villages in Greece.

Dating back to the Middle Ages, Stemnitsa is built in giddy tiers of lovely old stone houses up a precipice on the western slopes of Mount Mainelon at 1,100 metres. The village has a wonderful view down the long, deep Lousios Gorge. The main square is a quiet oasis of shops, tavernas and a church under tall plane trees. At the heart of all this is the popular *kafeneio,* the Gerousia, established in 1870. It's an elegant, traditional place with the typical line-up of old village photographs from the last two centuries, and you can tell the place really comes into its own in the winter, attracting locals and visitors with its cosy wood-burning fire. Sophia, the owner's mother, is very friendly and proud of the establishment, as it regularly features in Greek newspaper articles.

The *plateia* is classy and sedate – well it was until we arrived with Wallace, our Jack Russell terrier. We sat outside at one of the tables under the trees. Sophia was very taken with him, hiding sweetly under the table. Or, at least, acting sweet.

"He's very quiet," she said. But the minute her back was turned, Wallace bolted out from under the table like a mad cuckoo clock announcing the hour, and barked at an old Greek guy passing by, frightening the life out of him. When Sophia returned with our coffees and the local specialty *skaltsounia* (little socks), pastry shells filled with walnuts and honey, Wallace had skittered away again, which amused her.

"What's your little dog's name?" she asked.

"Wallakos," I told her, which is what the owner of the house we were renting in Koroni called him, and meaning 'Little Wallace'. Perhaps Sophia didn't hear me properly, or it was my pronunciation, but she burst into wild gusts of laughter. She shouted to an old guy in Greek, twiddling his worry beads nearby, "The dog's called Malakas! Can you believe it?"

"Not Malakas," I said, in hushed, offended tones. "Why would we call him that?" *Malakas* is a rude word in Greek, the least offensive translation being 'jerk', the worst 'wanker'. Wallace has been many things in his life. But malakas? Never!

"Oh, I'm sorry. I thought that's what you said," Sophia explained apologetically. But there was a twinge of amusement in her voice and she then had to explain to the old guy what Wallace's real name was. The man shrugged with Olympian verve and spun his worry beads a few times. Ha, *xenoi*, what are they like? his facial expression seemed to say.

It was amusing all the same, and as if to make amends Sophia gave us a small container of cherry tomatoes from her garden. "Not for now. To take away," she smiled, but insisted we try a couple to see how good they were. They didn't quite go with coffee and sweet pastries but we were used to Greeks and the way they combined things, any kind of things really. In one of the houses we rented in the Mani the owners often brought us odd gift combinations. Maria would knock at our front door, saying, "I have brought you firelighters and broccoli." Well, why not! But in any case, Sophia's tomatoes were very sweet and juicy.

Stemnitsa is rich in old-world charm, with some quirky rural corners – great towers of olive wood stacked for winter, donkeys tethered in gardens, gates and fences fashioned from long whittled bits of wood. It could have been a setting for a Brothers Grimm fairy tale, without all the scary stuff. The village is best appreciated by walking up the narrow streets, with their solid stone houses and stout wooden shutters built for cold weather. The village is also renowned for its gold and silver smithery and school. It was established in the 1970s, teaching the craft, and there are plenty of shops selling silver and gold jewellery.

There are 18 churches here, from the 12th century to 17th century, which is an amazing number for this rather remote village. You need to ask at the main square for the keyholders, who will probably be the local priests, and Sophia would be your go-to woman, I wager, for tracking them down, as long as you have the time and don't mind an occasional wild goose chase. The church in the main square, Ayios (Saint) Yiorgos, has a fine collection of 17th century frescos and is open most mornings.

There may be mischievous gods stalking this region, but there are also strange rural cults as well. Mount Lykaio (Wolf Mountain), in the west of Arcadia, which more fancifully is said to be the haunt of werewolves, makes the region seem a bit like Transylvania at times.

Arcadia is the vast central region of the Peloponnese, with its mountains, gorges, rivers, alpine forests and the city of Tripolis in the middle. It also has a long sea coast in the east and is bordered in the south by Messinia. The western side of the region, including Gortynia, is rich in ancient and natural attractions and gives a compact introduction to it. The archaeological site of Lykosoura is said to be the oldest 'city' in the world and even goat-legged Pan was thought to have had an oracle there. The ruined Temple of Despoina (the Mistress), a slipstream sister of the venerable Persephone, is said to date back to 180 BC. The women's dress code here, according to the Cadogan guide, is inscribed on the north side of the temple and states, "No provocative dress, no rings, no make-up and no fancy hairdos." It makes you wonder what a fancy hairdo would have looked like in the second century BC – maybe a messy up-do complete with writhing snakes.

The only place that mars the sense of mythical charm in this part of Arcadia is Megalopolis. A venerable city in ancient times, it's now most remembered for its modern power-generation plants. It's a vital industry here on the plain but the sight of giant smoke stacks belching out pollution on an Athenian scale is discouraging.

Mt Lykaio has sweeping views out over the southern Peloponnese and Taygetos mountains. It has a windswept Scottish highland feel about it, complete with bright-coloured thistles. But there the comparison ends. Although the walk to the top is recommended for its views, on the day we visited, on another occasion earlier in the summer, it was swelteringly hot and we had to forgo the trek. During the drive back to the plain we stopped the car and dashed to a natural spring water outlet, with marble surround, by the roadside, where the water was cold and sweet. We filled our water bottles and let Wallace sit in the marble bowl to cool his nether regions, which lightened the mood of several passing drivers, one of whom tooted his horn loudly.

Apart from its aura of bucolic charm and mischief, the area does have an ecclesiastical vibe, with three amazing monasteries built along the side of the deep Lousios gorge, particularly the monastery of Ayiou Ioanni Prodromou (St

John the Forerunner, or Baptist), which is one of the most curious and famous cliff-face monasteries in Greece. You can't see the establishment from the parking area at the top of the gorge as it's well hidden, but a sign sends you down a *kalderimi*, a cobbled path that leads down the side of the steep gorge, with a river gushing below.

Just when you think the monastery can't possibly be there and you've obviously missed a turning somewhere, because there's nothing but a steep-sided ravine, you look up and there it is, high above you. It's a precarious-looking spread of buildings clinging like limpets on a mossy cliff, under a thick lip of rock. It has a wide row of monks' cells with tiny balconies held up by wooden buttresses underneath. Above the *katholikon,* the monastery church, a long balcony provides a central focus of the monastery. From the roof of the balcony hang several bells that create a sweet sound that reverberates all along the gorge, which might have been the plan for gathering in monks, or chiming out a warning in more pugilistic centuries. But while the monks are sleeping or attending services, the area is deadly quiet, apart from the gush of the river far below.

Established in the 12th century, the monastery and its church, also built into the rockface with 16th century frescos inside, was a refuge for resistance fighters during the Greek War of Independence from 1821, and it also served as a hospital. At one time the monastery sheltered the superhero Kolokotronis. Born in Messinia in 1770, Kolokotronis was a clan chief and one of the leaders of the Messinian uprising against the Ottoman Turks that kicked off in Kalamata at the start of the War of Independence. He later went to the neighbouring village of Karitaina to raise troops for the battle and in 1825 made the old Karitaina castle his headquarters. Somehow during these years he was forced to take refuge at this monastery, with the Turks in pursuit, a not uncommon event during the war. The heavy studded door on the church is still riddled with bullet holes from these infamous and bloody sieges.

It is a curious fact that wherever you go, especially in the Mani, southern Peloponnese, you find innumerable locations reputed to have sheltered Kolokotronis. Sometimes you feel he's had more sightings than Elvis in his lifetime. Whatever historic castle, church or tower house you visit, Kolokotronis had always been in the building. However, so great was the adoration of this man that when he died in 1843 he was affectionately given the title of the 'the old man of the Morea', the latter being the ancient word for the Mani.

Arcadia is an enchanting place, a small corner of Greece that probably won't change much because of its mountainous terrain. On our way home we passed alluring Karitaina, where a late-afternoon mist added enchantment to the 13th century castle atop a conical-shaped hill that Kolokotronis occupied. The castle still has medieval cred and a swashbuckling history, seized by the French, Franks, Byzantines and Turks. It's massively atmospheric and lures you as you drive by. Perhaps it was the fault of Karitaina or minxy Pan and the drone of his pipes, but our sense of direction seemed to be blitzed and we ended up taking a duff turning that added another hour to the return journey to Koroni. Or was it some Arcadian spell to make sure you never leave?

15

Afraid of relics? Look away now!

I'VE found that often in life the anticipation of facing something strange or ghoulish is more frightening than the actual object itself – especially in a Greek church.

Ayios Yiorgos church, in the main square of Stemnitsa in Arcadia (mentioned in the previous chapter), has an extra attraction for the visitor apart from its wondrous frescos. It has a silver box containing a piece of bone reputed to have belonged to St Leontios, which is kept inside a glass case in the nave of the church.

Not much is known about this 18th century saint, apart from the fact he was born in Stemnitsa and later became a hermit in a cave on Mount Kastania, opposite the nearby village of Vlachera. He turned the cave into a small monastery over the years and was reputed to have done good deeds for locals and pilgrims. This old bone was tame compared to other relics I've had the misfortune to see in Greece.

It's not an uncommon practice in Greece to display holy relics in churches. A relic, or *leipsano*, can be anything from a piece of clothing belonging to a saint, a piece of bone, a body part, or even a whole body which has survived 'incorrupt', sometimes for many centuries, as proof of the saint's holy powers. Several Greek churches retain the bodies of saints: St Dionysus in Zakynthos, St Gerasimos in Kefalonia and St Spyridon in Corfu. Mystical powers of healing are attributed to many of the relics.

In Thessaloniki, the church of Ayios Dimitirios is named after the martyr saint who lived in the 4th century AD. He was killed when he tried to stand again Christian persecution and was buried in a crypt under what is now the present church. Some of his relics were found in 1917 and placed in a small casket. St Dimitrios has been given the bizarre name of the 'Myrrhgusher' because every year on his feast day when the casket is opened during the church service, myrrh (a perfumed resin used from ancient times) is said to flow from the inside. The coffee-coloured liquid is collected by the faithful and fills the church with a remarkable fragrance.

Relics are venerated in Greece, along with icons. The Orthodox Christians believe, as do Roman Catholics, that relics play a significant role. Timothy Ware, in his book *The Orthodox Church*, says, "... they believe that the grace of God, present in the saints' bodies during life, remains active in their relics when they have died and that God uses these relics as a channel of divine power and an instrument of healing."

On the feast days of saints whose relics are kept in church, they will be brought out and venerated in the liturgy and the congregation is invited to kiss them and offer an intercessory prayer for themselves or someone in need. Depending on your religious beliefs, it's either a blessing to venerate a holy relic or it's something you don't want to repeat in a hurry. I fall into the latter category.

I was in Corfu town in 1980 on holiday and not particularly knowledgeable then about the intricacies of the Orthodox faith. I found myself outside the Church of St Spyridon, the patron saint of the island, whose skeletal remains lie in a long gold-plated reliquary box inside a silver casket in the church. Several times a year the casket is opened and the reliquary is laid out so that devotees may pay homage to the saint and seek a blessing, and the reliquary is then carried in a procession by priests around the town. I'd only been in Corfu a few days and it had slipped my mind that this momentous occasion was coming up, and that it was also the official feast day of this saint.

The street outside was crowded and somehow I was propelled inside the church by a great force of people, like an ecclesiastical conga line, from which there was no way out. The atmosphere inside was electric, or hysterical, whichever way you look at these things. I found myself in a kind of queue heading towards a side chapel and the church was now too packed for me to consider any kind of orderly retreat. In the chapel a *papas*, priest, stood at the head of the reliquary, performing a liturgy with an orderly beside him swinging a censer, the small room filling up with fragrant but choking incense.

"What's happening here?" I whispered hoarsely to a genial-looking woman in front of me.

She explained that we were all waiting to kiss the relics of St Spyridon, for whom the reliquary had been designed with a large square cut-out at the top. Judging by some of the postcards I'd seen in kiosks about town, this would reveal the saint's actual head – not a pretty sight and decidedly relic-y, given that it was nearly 1,700 years old.

Holy Hell! I thought. I've always enjoyed Orthodox services, even in those early days of my travels round Greece, when I knew little about them. I love the aura inside a Greek church: the muted light, the darkened corners, the frescos with ranks of august-looking saints, the incense and the chanting. It's a feeling of being somewhere totally outside your normal experience of life, somewhere rarefied, closer to God if you like.

A *papas* in Kalamata once explained to me that the Orthodox service is special because it affects all your senses at once, and therein lies its great power and attraction. And venerating/kissing the icons is a fundamental part of the ritual, especially the icon dedicated to the saint after whom the church is named. I have held back from kissing them directly, not after several hundred other people have just smooched them. Think of the bacteria! Even today, in an era of showy air-kissing, which was generally not an option in Greek churches in earlier decades, I still flinch a bit. But smooching the actual relics is another matter entirely. The neat freak inside me really kicks in then.

Which is why, when I was nearly at the head of the Spyridon queue, I started sweating and having a ridiculous kind of panic attack. The incense seemed to be devouring oxygen, the light was bright and achy, reflecting off the highly ornamented reliquary and a chandelier hanging above. I started to get floaters in my eyes. I watched as each devotee took their place, bending down to the saint's head, kissing it, mumbling and crossing themselves. I felt queasy and faint. I grabbed the arm of the kindly woman in front of me and held on. If I was going down on the marble floor, she was coming with me.

It wasn't that I didn't think of the indignity and unseemly razzmatazz that this ancient saint was put through like this, several times a year, during various other celebrations. Born in 348 AD in his native Cyprus, St Spyridon quickly showed himself to be devout and something of a miracle worker. He was said to have once – to prove a point of faith to his followers – picked up a pot shard from the ground and made it burst into flames, which is why in his Orthodox icon he is often depicted holding a flaming pot shard in his right hand. You couldn't really make it up, could you?

When he died his 'incorrupted' relics, or in his case his body, survived down the centuries, proving his saintly status, and they were allegedly the source of many further miracles among his devotes. Even after death the saint had a peripatetic, busy life, with his body taken to Constantinople for safe-keeping. But in 1452, the year before the city, then part of the Roman Empire, fell to the Ottoman Turks, the saint was moved to a female monastery outside the city, and then to the Church of the Holy Apostles.

Late in the 15th century it was decided to send his body to Greece, a safer location. There are several stories of how this was accomplished. My favourite is the slightly bizarre one that he was transported to Greece in a straw-filled sack loaded on to a donkey, which I favour over some of the other more stitched-up tales of transportation by a bevy of dignitaries sent from Italy.

His body ended up in Corfu, and was traipsed about a lot more to various churches on the island until the head of a distinguished local family built a church especially for the saint in Corfu town in 1527. The centuries of globetrotting had been fiendishly wearing and along the way St Spyridon lost his right arm, which was said to have turned up – miraculously – in Rome sometime after the 16th century, where it was held in a small casket and not returned to St Spyridon in his Corfiot church until the 1980s.

He became Corfu's patron saint because prayers to him at certain tumultuous times in Corfu's history were claimed to have saved the island. In 1629, when a plague ripped through Corfu, prayers were offered by the islanders which stopped the spread of the plague within three days, after which it never reappeared, something we could perhaps emulate in these Covid-19 disaster days of 2020/1.

So this was not a saint to be taken lightly and as I waited panicky in the queue for my 'turn' at the saint's reliquary, I wondered what state this poor guy would be in now, with a couple more centuries under his belt since he arrived here. And I was about to find out. Once the Greek woman in front had unpinned me from her arm she performed her veneration, and then I was propelled to the head of the reliquary by the antsy queue behind. Even today I can remember the light in that chapel, the clamour, the tired gimlet eyes of the *papas*, the musty smell. It was the stuff of the old Hammer horror films – to me anyway.

Okay, I thought, I'll just go up and fake a kiss and avert my gaze. And there he was below me before I could say 'run like the wind'. The sight was like the postcard images but worse: a gruesome dark grey face below the cut-out, a cap of sorts on his head, a strange bashed nose, an open mouth, as if midway through a muted scream, silenced forever, and a few teeth. But what I didn't expect was the way his head tilted awkwardly to the left, as if he was eternally tired, or his head had somehow become detached since the rest of the 'body' lay hidden which, given the history of the relic, would have been no surprise.

What I felt in the end was not horror but, strangely, pity. I felt sorry for this poor guy and the indignity of having to stay in the public glare forever more, something that none of us would want, saint or not. But to kiss, or not to kiss, that was the question. That's when I noticed the plexiglass screen across the top of the reliquary cut-out, set lower than its rim. Oh, for God's sake, I thought, with a sigh of relief! Why hadn't I factored that in? The glass was kiss-smudged, with the odd scarlet lipstick pucker. I air-kissed the glass from a great height and pushed my way out of the chapel, and out of the church, elbowing anyone who thwarted my flight.

Like a small rocket I landed outside on the road, gulping in the sweet cool air. I even managed to laugh at myself, at my own stupidity and blind panic, all the way to a nearby *kafeneio* for a soothing glass or two of something strong.

Despite my funk over relics, to this day, whenever I visit a church displaying them, like the one in Stemnitsa square, I simply have to go and look. How bad can it be? A finger, a toe, a nib of nose? Once you've gazed into St Spyridon's sad grey physiognomy you can look at almost anything.

16

The high road to happiness

"I CAN only wonder what it must be like to divest yourself of everything and take off into the wild blue yonder," a friend wrote to me when I told him of our impending trip to Greece in 2010.

As a medical professional with two young children in Sydney, his comment was motivated mainly by a wish to be free of daily pressures for a while, nothing more complicated than that. But many other friends said very similar things as we moved closer to our departure date. One writer friend with an interesting but insecure job and children to support complained rather mournfully, "Where is our mid-life odyssey? When can we do what you're doing?"

I felt for his predicament then, and would more so now in 2021, with the pandemic still seriously restricting all our lives and making something as fantastic as a long overseas odyssey near impossible – until a vaccine has been rolled out globally. Even then, travel might not be the same as it was, with health passports and restrictions on those from Covid-19 hotspots.

Even back in 2010, cutting loose for a long adventure abroad wasn't always easy. But all the same, I told my friend, "You can do it one day if you really want it badly enough." And that became our stock answer to those laments, because that statement had been true for us.

We had put in a huge amount of planning and time into the proposed odyssey, putting our personal possessions into storage, renting out our apartment in Scotland, as well as all the bureaucratic issues involved in leaving the UK for a while. Our to-do list before we left, including a pet passport and microchip for our dog Wallace, was four A4 pages long and took us weeks to work through. But not once did we doubt we were doing the right thing, even though Greece was moving into the first stages of its economic crisis and was securing a massive bailout from the EU, with no signs of how the country would survive.

We wanted it badly enough, but we didn't seek out the odyssey because we hated our lives, or where we lived. We had a pleasant life in a picturesque village outside Stirling, set on a trickling stream with a famous castle perched above on a flank of the Ochil hills. It was all very Brigadoonish. The main reason we wanted to leave – apart from an Arctic winter and some career frustrations – was that we aimed to live for a while under a 'wandering star'. And who doesn't?

But sadly, the subtext to a lot of the comments we heard repeatedly from those to whom we explained our plans was that many Brits were desperate for an overseas odyssey, or in some cases a permanent move abroad, because they were fed up with their lives in the UK. They were chasing the elusive, dream-life-in-the-sun fantasy that has been promoted for a few decades now on British TV and social media, and still is. However, in 2021, in the midst of the terrible Covid-19 pandemic, the fantasy seems redundant for now and even a bit cliché and tired. Until now, people have been lured into thinking that life could be much happier if only they were somewhere else, anywhere other than Blighty.

But is this true? Notwithstanding the restrictions of our new 'normal' lives, can you be happier just because you change location, especially to a sunny country like Greece? I don't think so. It will be different, for sure, but not necessarily happier or better. We knew this already, having lived in Australia for years and having made a much more challenging move back to Britain in 2000 that seemed like a *Ben Hur* production at the time.

Our years in Greece brought us in contact with many British, American and other expatriates, who told us they went to live in Greece to 'escape' their old humdrum lives and, in many cases, personal disasters such as bankruptcy, flagrant infidelities, divorce. The list was endless!

Many of them obviously thrived in the gorgeous Greek climate, with a better lifestyle than they had back home, particularly the Brits, as if they were permanently on holiday. No-one should blame them, particularly pensioners, for wanting easier lives and sun and sea. Many confessed to being happier in their new location, and said it was the best move they'd ever made. However, those who sought Greece for a particular reason rather than the expectation of just being happier and living a nebulous dream, were probably the most successful resettlers, especially those who managed to assimilate well.

The American artist and writer Pamela Jane Rogers left the US for a complete change of scene and ended up settling permanently on Poros island. She has been living there for more than 30 years. She mainly went to Greece for its beauty and as an inspiration for her painting. She's one of the success stories, building up a great reputation for her work worldwide and she has written a fascinating memoir about her life in Greece, *Greekscapes: Journeys With An Artist.* Many other writers and artists also find that Greece provides a less conventional and sunny muse and they have no intention of leaving.

However, a move to Greece is not always the answer to everything. Some British expats told us that although their lifestyle was easier, they were shocked to discover they weren't as happy as they thought they would be. The same problems that plagued them back home plagued them in Greece, and in Greece there was less of a safety net: a poorer health system, frustrating bureaucracy, and their extended families were not around for support.

Many of those who escaped to Greece have ultimately returned home. One expat I interviewed for a British newspaper feature in 2010 went to Greece with her husband, where they built their 'dream home' on a hillside behind Kalamata. But it turned out to be anything but. After a heartbreaking saga with disreputable builders, bureaucracy and other disasters, including a hideous rat infestation, they sold up and moved back reluctantly to the UK, and have no further plans to pursue a dream life abroad.

A few other British couples we met had sadly left their dream of moving abroad too late in life and by the time the houses were bought or built and the business of dealing with bureaucracy and the slew of new taxes during the crisis was dealt with, they were struck with serious ill-health that required a quick return to Britain and the sale of their house, often with all its contents. It's a tragic consequence of moving abroad that no-one wants to face.

One of the most peculiar relocation stories I've ever heard came from the Messinian peninsula, told to us by some local expats. A rather pleasant but reclusive English couple had bought a large and pleasant house near Koroni, with lovely views down to the gulf. They lived there for several years before deciding that Greek life wasn't for them. They sold up, went back to England, to the region they'd come from originally, and bought a house there. But after a few years they hated life back home, the weather and everything they'd initially run away from. So, remarkably, they sold up once more and went back to Koroni to house hunt. However, nothing they saw compared to the first house they'd owned there and they rented for a while. When their original house unexpectedly came up for sale, they bought it *again*, paying more than they had in the first place!

It might seem like complete madness but it shows that sometimes you need to lose a thing to appreciate it. But that may not be all they lost. As a shrewd English friend, who ran a real estate business in Kalamata, once remarked, "Some expats when they come to Greece leave their brains behind on the baggage carousel." I felt sorry for the Koroni couple but imagined that they had not thought out the original move to Greece in much detail, or what they wanted from the country.

These stories revealed one thing to me: that you can't ramp up happiness just by changing location, even if it's a location you think you love and understand. A new perspective might be a skewed perspective. Happiness isn't a greener square of lawn. It's something deeper, more intrinsic. There's a line in a poem by famous Greek poet Konstantinos Kavafis that sums it up. It loosely translates as, "You can change your skies but not your soul."

To a great extent that's true. The old life will follow you about wherever you go. A broken heart will be a broken heart wherever you are. A failure to relate to others, or to feel fulfilled on many levels, won't change just because you go to Greece, or another sunny location. You won't live longer, or feel younger, just because you've chased a dream life. And you won't be more interesting just because you've stepped away from the disgruntled masses in your place of birth.

Conversely, if you are truly happy and healthy within yourself to start with, then it doesn't matter whether you live in Grimsby or Greece.

The expats we often met in Greece were searching for different things, and sometimes it wasn't always as straightforward as they'd imagined. And neither was it for us. We never left in search of the 'dream life in the sun'. Who could even do that in Greece as it tumbled into a desperate economic crisis that quickly became a humanitarian disaster after a year or two: penury, social chaos, unemployment and disgrace on a huge scale, which changed Greek life forever. It would have seemed callous for foreigners to search out a dream life while everyone else's was slipping into the maelstrom.

We initially left for an adventure in Greece because we loved the location for what it was. We wanted to be able to experience and write about it as journalists and also earn a living. As someone who has been visiting Greece all my life, sometimes for long periods of time, I had confidence in Greek people, and knew that in the midst of social ferment, they would be characteristically inclusive and kind, and that we would survive there.

As one year ran into four, we became settled and more seduced by the place. However, I can't say that life in Greece in the crisis years was easy. Far from it, and there were times – especially in 2012 when austerity measures were at their worst and some Greek commentators were calling it "the slow death of Greece" – when we seriously considered whether it might be time to return to Scotland. And yet we didn't because whatever had drawn us to Greece in the first place still had a strong grip.

But what is the lure, for Greece in particular? The issue came to have a bit more significance one spring day in the Mani while we were guests at a village celebration. A slightly cynical Greek businessman called Tasos and I had been chatting about our Greek adventure.

"Why did you pick this poor time to come to our country for an adventure my friends?" he asked, looking bemused. Caught off-guard, I made a vague response about the weather, the beaches, the pleasant lifestyle.

"Maybe, but if that's the case, there are sunnier and easier places in the world to live than Greece. Like Spain, for instance."

I felt there was a mild criticism implied of expats in Greece, and a little xenophobia perhaps. I told Tasos I had no interest in living in Spain and that I had always felt drawn to Greece for various reasons.

"Everyone is," he said, with a shrug, not satisfied I thought with my response.

"But apart from sun and sea, what do you really seek to find, my friends, in our country that you cannot find in your own? Forgive me, I mean no insult."

I didn't find Tasos a sympathetic character really but it was a good question, and very perceptive. It was something I thought about a great deal during those years in Greece: the illusive thing we're all seeking there in a culture more complex and alien than our own, notwithstanding the hospitality and kindness of Greeks. I'm not sure if I found the answer or not. Or that it can be found.

Jim and I went to Greece for an exciting break, for a temporary reset of our lives, but I don't believe we went seeking, or feeling entitled to, greater happiness and contentment, or the fanciful notion of the 'dream life'. However, I think we were unintentionally happier overall during our Greek years, despite the fact that not all our experiences were positive. We didn't always get things right. We had tough times in the crisis, like everyone. We found it hard adjusting to a very traditional rural culture that was often raw and uncompromising and often took us beyond what we found comfortable and normal.

However, we went to Greece without any illusions or expectations and so were constantly surprised and delighted by everything we found, helped in no small part by the wonderful Greeks we met (and occasionally expats, too), who shared their lives and their stories. Because we never sought happiness in a different location, I believe we found it and therein may be one of the few things we learnt after four years in Greece. Perhaps we had, unintentionally, absorbed the easy Greek philosophy of living in the moment – for what it is, and not what we need or want it to be; of living contentedly with much less.

The expat I mentioned earlier, whose dream house near Kalamata became the house from hell, told me that when she finally settled back in Britain, she realised perhaps for the first time what positive things her own country had to offer, such as laws to protect people, on the whole, from unscrupulous builders and landlords, along with things like health and safety and animal rights. And that misdemeanours have consequences, which they don't always have in Greece. These were things she'd never considered before about her own society but was now extremely grateful for. Decent pest control also came high on her list, given the location of her Greek house on the rat run from hell! So her story had a happy ending after all.

Of course, even in the new normal, with the Covid virus perhaps hovering somewhere in the background, there's still a case for going abroad to seek another kind of life, or to have a long adventure if possible. Yet I would say that if you embark on that long-coveted odyssey, don't go expecting it will change your life forever. As Kavafis indicated, it may only change your 'sky' and nothing more – unless that's really all you want. And if it is, you're truly blessed.

17

Uncovering my father's war

SOMETIMES reality has a way of imitating fiction – and not the other way round. In my case, this happened a few months after publishing my first novel, *A Saint For The Summer,* and what I discovered has changed the way I look at my family history forever. The novel is a contemporary story set in the Mani region of southern Greece but with a narrative thread going back to the Second World War in Kalamata.

The book follows the story of Scottish journalist Bronte McKnight, who goes to Greece to help her expat father Angus solve a mystery from the war, when his father Kieran, serving in Greece with the Royal Army Service Corps, went missing in the Battle of Kalamata. This disastrous battle in

1941 has been called the 'Greek Dunkirk', when around 10,000 British and allied soldiers, retreating from the German advance in central Greece, ended up in Kalamata, the 'end of the road', and were left stranded on the city's beach at the head of the Messinian Gulf. The novel follows the exciting but difficult path Angus and Bronte take, with few leads, to search out what became of Kieran and where he was buried, helped by a cast of Greek characters.

I became curious about the Battle of Kalamata while living in this southern region partly because it had a huge impact there and yet, beyond Greece, it was almost unknown. While researching it, I did think of my own father, John McGinn, who served in WW2 in the RAF Regiment, which was a specialist airfield defence corps formed in 1942. I knew he had been deployed to North Africa and Italy, for which he received medals, but I knew very little about what specific conflicts he was involved in and his experiences. I didn't base *Saint* on his war experience, and as far as I knew then he hadn't been sent to Greece. However, I did base Kieran's personality and his Celtic looks on my father, who had magnificent wavy auburn hair and fine bone structure. He was a handsome young man, full of high spirits, with Irish and Scottish roots.

Writing the novel had been a fairly intense undertaking, so after it was published I took a summer break from writing. Yet I couldn't quite get the WW2 aspects of the story out of my mind. Curiously, it brought my thoughts back to my father again and made me wonder about his own war exploits. I knew so little. As a kid, I used to ask him for his war stories and he always flinched, saying he couldn't talk about it, and I accepted that it was something he preferred to forget.

As he died a long while ago, and was estranged from much of his family when we moved from Scotland to Australia in the 1960s, I had no way of finding out any more. A search online a few years ago for his war record yielded nothing, as

I didn't have his squadron number for one thing. Or so I thought. I had a fine collection of old family photos and a mass of memorabilia that had been in storage for some years. I promised myself I would sift through it properly once I took a break from travelling and writing books. It was now time to get started.

After sorting through the documents, I came across a faded newspaper photo of a few regiment men, including my father, squatting behind a mortar gun, but I had no idea when or where it was taken. There were also photocopies of two seasonal RAF telegrams from my father to his family back in Scotland in 1943 and 44. They were small with tiny cramped handwriting across the top, the first illustrated with a palm tree from "LAC (Leading Aircraftman) McGinn" to his family wishing them a Merry Christmas, presumably from Africa. The second had a map of the Mediterranean and was also a Christmas telegram. I was just able to make out his service and squadron numbers, however, which was invaluable.

With this information, I went online to try to find out anything about the exploits of this squadron. Fortunately, there is now a lot more war information online than in previous years and the amount of material uploaded (eyewitness accounts, journals) from the two world wars grows all the time.

It was online that I had a breakthrough. And oddly enough it was this factor of being able to search for vital war information on the internet that had been a pivotal part of *Saint* when the fictional father Angus tracks down a possible pointer to the disappeared Kieran on an online war site. The reason for this inclusion in the plot was because in Greece I had come across several expats researching the Battle of Kalamata and lost relatives who had done something similar and it had impressed me. So in effect, I was, without really meaning to, following my own fictional plot.

In researching my father I found several sites with accounts of the war exploits of his 2771 Squadron, particularly in Italy in 1944, and some of the information was taken from a book published in 2013, *RAF Regiment at War 1942 to 46* by Kingsley Oliver, which for me has proved invaluable. I was able to establish for the first time what my father's squadron at least had done in Italy, which gave me huge reverence for his war experience and explained why he hadn't wanted to talk about it.

I also had the amazing good fortune of finding photos online of the squadron taken during the battle of Monte Cassino in Italy. On one site, I recognised the original photo of the newspaper clipping my father had kept all those years of him and three other men in a mortar crew and it transpired my father was the crew commander of the small group. That find led to the discovery of other photos, all taken by an official war photographer in Monte Cassino, including one of my father standing in allied 'headquarters', an archway under the Colle Belvedere aqueduct north of Cassino. It was firm proof of where he had been during the Italian campaign. And there was another surprise at the end of my research that I was wasn't expecting (more of that later).

The squadron had initially been deployed to North Africa and after the surrender there of the Axis powers in 1943, they were sent off to the Italian campaign against the occupying German forces. They went first to Naples and Rimini and in the spring of 1944 to the front line, not far from Monte Cassino. The Battle of Monte Cassino was four assaults by the allies on a strategic part of the German-held 'Gustave Line' that crossed the rugged terrain of southern Italy, with the aim of forcing the Germans to retreat, and to protect the route to Rome.

These were among the fiercest and bloodiest engagements of the war in Western Europe, involving French, American and British forces, along with its allies: Indians, New Zealanders and Poles. Because of the intractable terrain, which included rivers and ravines, some of the British troops dubbed the area The Inferno. The battles here were comparable to some of the worst scenes of WW1, with 55,000 allied casualties. The RAF Regiment was there in a support role, alongside other British regiments on the front line. One of the other aircraftmen in the 2771 squadron, Corporal Alf Blackett, who would have fought alongside my father, later wrote of his wartime experiences in Cassino and the relentless fighting.

"It's a grim life, clinging tenaciously to the side of a steep hill with the Germans in strength on the other side and the RAF Regiment men holding a sector of the front line." At one point during an assault he said, "The regiment moved up to their positions on a moonless night in their tin hats and khaki. Near to the front, the officer told them to smoke their last cigarette. 'This, chaps, is going to be one mad ride'."

One eyewitness described it as a 'living hell', with the wounded and dead ferried down the hill in the 'Death Wagon'. The hill was a strategic point in the battle, with a monastery at the top that was held by the Germans and was the target of much of the bombing. Although the allied forces were victorious in driving the Germans away from the Gustav Line in this decisive battle for Italy, I began to understand why my father had never had the stomach to talk about Monte Cassino.

In the pages of his squadron's Operations Record Books, copies of which were given to me by an RAF Regiment historian, it reports horrendous exchanges of bombing and mortar fire every day for most of May 1944, with more than 60 mortars fired in one night alone towards enemy positions. While my father survived the hell of Cassino without being badly wounded, as part of the Regiment's mortar crew the constant firing and enemy bombardments on the front line destroyed much of his hearing, which was a disability that affected him for the rest of his life.

But the greatest surprise to me from my research into the operations of 2771 Squadron is that after the Cassino engagement ended by June 1944, the squadron was deployed to Greece in December after the German withdrawal from the country. Some British forces, including the RAF Regiment, were there to provide airfield protection at the Araxos base in the north-west Peloponnese. They were also there "for duty in connection with political disturbance", in other words to help in supporting Greek government troops who were fighting the communists, particularly the military arm of EAM (National Liberation Front) and the KKE, the Greek communist party, at the start of the Greek civil war which continued until 1949.

The 2771 Squadron helped to defend the Hassani airfield, an RAF base south of Athens, which during the war had been used as a Luftwaffe base. The squadron was also tasked with supporting British ground forces in central Athens against communist attacks, and left Greece early the following year when Athens was secured. His squadron was redeployed to Yugoslavia during the spring.

My father, as far as I remember, had never mentioned his time in Greece, but the fact his squadron had been there was a huge revelation to me. From a personal point of view, Greece has always been a driving force in my life from my childhood. As a newly arrived Scottish migrant to Australia in the 1960s, I was befriended by a Greek girl at my school – my first real friend. Over the years, I became almost part of her extended family. After leaving school, I travelled through Europe to Athens to work for a year and have visited Greece numerous times, culminating in my recent four-year stint.

In all that time I had no idea that my father's war postings may have taken him there. For me to have written a novel with a Scottish soldier lost in the Battle of Kalamata, in Greece, whom I decided to create in my father's likeness, seems incredible to me now. It's as if the strands of our lives had become woven together at strategic points and mirrored each other's, although I never knew that until recently.

When I see old photos of my father after he signed up to the RAF Regiment, he looked so young and full of enthusiasm. Aged 19 and a *gallus* young lad (daring, high-spirited), it would have seemed in the beginning like a grand adventure into the unknown, something I could relate to. The fact he had his 21st birthday on the front line in Monte Cassino adds extra poignancy to this part of his life. Did he raise a glass of anything to celebrate, so young and far from home? Did there seem like anything worth celebrating? It was another aspect of his life he never spoke about.

However, my father was no stranger to hard times. Born in a rundown tenement in the infamous east end of Glasgow, the second oldest in a large family, living in a couple of draughty rooms, the war for him was – as for many working-class British kids – transformative. When I was a curious youngster seeking his war stories he at least told me, "It was an escape from poverty." Yet it turned into a descent into the inferno in Italy. At least he survived and eventually had his 'dream life' in sunny Australia.

And my research goes on. As I write, I am still waiting for a detailed report into my father's war service. But even when I finally have a more complete idea of my father's time during WW2, there will always be stories and details I will never know, sadly. Had I not written my first novel with its WW2 strand, it's quite possible I may not have felt the urge to dig further into my father's war record. I'm certainly glad I did because I now know and understand much more about my father's early life. And the fact that my book and his life are now intertwined on some level has touched me greatly.

18

Losing our Marbles?

ON a bitterly cold winter day, I was standing in front of a stately home called Broomhall House in central Scotland, wondering how I could blag my way inside. Why bother? Well, amazingly, this grey, slightly dour pile in the midst of the Fife countryside was no ordinary stately home, but the catalyst for one of the most contentious cultural heists in history. And within its walls there were secrets that had never been winkled out, which piqued my journalistic curiosity.

The house, near the village of Charlestown, is the family seat of the Earls of Elgin. It was redesigned in 1798 for Thomas Bruce, the 7th Earl of Elgin, in the Greek revivalist style. Lord Elgin was best known for his infamous heist of the Parthenon sculptures, popularly known as the 'Elgin Marbles', most of which he planned to adorn Broomhall House with on his return to Scotland in the early 19th century. The haul amounted to nearly half of the sculptures and other carvings the Parthenon was decorated with at that time, as well as other significant items from the Acropolis.

Elgin's plan to install them in his Fife home was scuppered, however, when he returned from Greece after his stint as Ambassador to Constantinople. He was ill and broke and was forced to put the best of the antiquities up for sale. They were bought by the British Government and given over to the British Museum. Yet a small cache of them were kept in Broomhall House, a fact that isn't much talked about in Scotland, mainly because few people know about this collection of antiquities – and that's probably how the Elgin family like it.

While we were back in Scotland in 2014, after several years in Greece, I'd heard that the current head of the dynasty, Andrew Bruce, the 11th Earl of Elgin, still retained the Greek treasures inside the Fife house, and I decided to write about it. I planned to contact the family, as the house isn't normally open to the public, to see if I could get an invitation to look at the antiquities there. An ambitious plan, I confess. At that time, the debate over the sculptures and why they should be returned to Athens had fired up yet again, with various international celebrities co-opted into helping publicise the matter.

The subject was very much in our minds as well. Before we left Greece, Jim and I had visited the new Acropolis Museum in Athens to see the Parthenon sculptures. They are on display in the purpose-built top-floor gallery of this outstanding museum, with panoramic views of the Acropolis through its vast glass walls. Even if you weren't interested in the subject before, you couldn't help but have an opinion about the Elgin heist once you've seen what's left of the sculptures – fewer than half of them.

For the planned story, I rang an Edinburgh property management company that seemed the only point of contact for the Elgin family. Messages to the company about a visit went unanswered, so I left a voicemail message requesting a comment at least about the family's current collection of antiquities. No response. I later managed to winkle out of a local contact the phone number for Broomhall House and when the phone was finally picked up I was told, by what appeared to be a maid, that the family would not agree to speak about the 'Marbles' – ever! And that's pretty much the situation still.

Undeterred, I decided to go to the house and, if possible, doorstep the Elgins for a comment. As you do! It was easy to park nearby but after a short walk to the front of the house, I discovered the place was thoroughly roped off to the public and you couldn't get near it, never mind the front door. I made another call to the house number I'd used before, to state my interest here, but all I got was the answer phone. I left a message and number. I told them I was outside. I waved! And waited. Unsurprisingly, I didn't get a call back.

Broomhall House is an impressive pile on a vast 2,500-acre estate. It has an imposing revivalist frontage, with columns at the entrance, large windows, but Downton Abbey it is not! It looks cold and forbidding, and from a distance the irony of the whole 'Marbles' debate really kicks in. It's hard to fathom the aristocratic folly of the 7th Lord Elgin, or the hubris in wanting to hack apart one of Greece's great cultural achievements, and take some of the most admired antiquities in the world to create a kind of Caledonian Parthenon in a dour corner of rural Scotland.

In 1799, Lord Elgin was British Ambassador to Constantinople, under the Ottoman Empire, which ruled Greece at the time. While in Greece it is said he became obsessed with the Parthenon sculptures, created by the renowned sculptor Phidias using prized Pentelic marble in the 5th century BC, during the Golden Age of Greek civilization. It was built as a temple to the goddess Athena. Elgin was allegedly given permission by the Ottoman Turks in an official 'firman' to remove some sculptures from the Parthenon, though even the Turks were said to be later surprised by the number Elgin eventually took, employing hundreds of men to pull them down, many of which were smashed in the process. Academics and legal experts continue to argue over the existence of this 'firman', however, and therefore over the legitimacy of Elgin's actions.

Elgin took around 220 tonnes of sculptures and other items and it was all bound for Broomhall House, and financed by his wealthy Scottish heiress wife, Mary Nisbet. In 1801, Elgin had written to Italian landscape painter Giovanni Battista Lusieri, offering him work in Greece as the resident artist, capturing images of the sculptures, but in effect he also helped in the removal. Elgin said to Lusieri with self-importance, "I wish to collect as much marble as possible. I have places in my house which need it."

For this monumental frenzy of home furnishing, Elgin swiped 17 stunning life-sized statues from the pediments (gable ends) of the Parthenon, depicting the Olympian gods and goddesses and their struggles. These include some of the best of the statues: Helios, Dionysus, Artemis, Hestia and Aphrodite. The other sculptures taken were large carved metopes, which sat above the Parthenon columns, and half the frieze from its inner colonnade, which depicts a religious procession.

It would be divine justice perhaps to think there was a curse on Lord Elgin because after he finally left Greece nothing went right for him. At least one of the shipments of antiquities sank off the Ionian islands and it took several years for them to be salvaged. He arrived back in Britain in poor health with syphilis, and his wife duly divorced him. Then he discovered he was completely skint. He had to forget the folly of recreating the Parthenon in his stately home and was forced to sell the sculptures to the British Government in an Act of Parliament in 1816 for £35,000 (about £3.5 million today) – half of what he wanted.

Interestingly, it has been reported that during the sale there was never any request to see the official 'firman', if it ever really existed. Elgin's own justification for the heist was that he wished to preserve the items for posterity because the Acropolis in the 18th century had become a seedy garrison, with Turks using the antiquities for target practice.

While this is partly true, the sculptures, after being shipped from Athens, had a worse fate. They were stored by Elgin in a damp shed in central London for years before they were given to the British Museum and later they were over-cleaned and bleached by over-zealous BM staff. But the theft of the sculptures and subsequent treatment at least outraged many influential people in Britain at the time and English poet Lord Byron helped lead the charge. He wrote on the rock surrounding the Parthenon, "What the Goths spared, the Scots destroyed."

The Greeks have a passionate desire to see the sculptures returned to Athens, especially since part of the reason for building the new Acropolis Museum was to ultimately house all of these pieces in one place. There has been a groundswell of international support for the past 10 years, with celebrities coming on board, such as British actor/writer Stephen Fry and Hollywood star George Clooney and his human rights lawyer wife, Amal, who was acting as an adviser in 2014 to the Greek government in its bid to have the sculptures returned.

The collection held at Broomhall House would also be very welcome back in Greece. These were items the BM reportedly said were too small, damaged or insignificant to be included in the 1816 sale, but nevertheless the items are said to include important pieces of sculpture and grave markers (stelae) and other items. Yet very few people really know what the Broomhall collection contains. The current Earl of Elgin is a well-connected aristocrat, Eton-educated, a freemason and wealthy from farming. He will never need to part with his collection.

A picture taken in 1998, which I have seen, of the current Earl of Elgin (Andrew Bruce) in his study (from a story in *Freemasonry Today* magazine), shows what appears to be some items from the collection: a carved stele and some other marble pieces mounted on the wall behind him. Slim pickings compared to what his forebear looted, but for the Greeks these are all significant items. As the 7th Lord Elgin once said to his artist friend Lusieri, "The slightest item from the Acropolis is a jewel."

While researching this story, one local journalist I spoke to in the nearby village of Limekilns, Fife, who asked not to be named, told me he had been inside the house to interview the current Earl and that there were many antiquities lying about.

"They are all around the house, scattered informally like bits of the furniture, but they are quite striking. The Earl of Elgin will give you the history of the items, though I can't claim to really know their significance. His attitude to them is very relaxed and open because he doesn't feel he has anything to hide. What he will say is that he agrees with the 7th Lord Elgin in that they were brought to Britain for preservation, and that's what he's been brought up to think. The Elgin family are very close to the (British) Royal Family and they just have a different way of looking at things," he said.

Another local man I spoke to, a crusading retiree from Dunfermline who grew up near Broomhall House, has been researching and writing about the sculptures for a decade.

He said, "I believe there could be a lot more of the original pieces inside the house, especially smaller pieces because there was so much material taken from Athens, like funerary urns and items taken from the graves of some of Athens' greatest heroes."

Certainly there are antiquities that appear to be unaccounted for. A Fife library I contacted gave me a copy of a document dated 1810 with an inventory of Elgin's "Museum" (the sculptures etc) that predates the list of items presented at a parliamentary debate in 1816 before the items were bought and given to the BM. Some items on the 1810 list are not in the later one, like a large sarcophagus from Athens. Also, in a phone call to the BM I was told some items supposedly on the 1816 list are unaccounted for at the BM, as far as they know, such as three ancient cedar wood musical instruments, including a lute, taken from an Athens location. Where are they now?

There are those who would say that no-one should hold the present Earl of Elgin, aged 96, responsible for the sins of his forebear, or begrudge him the ownership of some of the antiquities. The Earl fought valiantly in the Royal Navy at the Normandy landing in 1944, where he was wounded. However, with increasing calls for reunification of the Parthenon art works, perhaps it's the right time for someone else in the Elgin family to engage in the argument.

As a member of Britain's upper class, and a proud Scot who can trace his ancestry back to Robert the Bruce, who secured Scottish independence from the English at the Battle of Bannockburn in 1314, the Earl's voice might carry influence. It might also lead the charge for the BM to hand over its collection because until now the museum has been intransigent on the subject.

Each successive UK government has also dug in its heels, saying the sculptures must remain in the BM, where it believes they are better looked after, even though the Acropolis Museum in Athens has an excellent gallery and state-of-the-art restoration techniques.

It seems nonsensical for the BM to keep its half of the sculptures. For example, on a recent visit to the Greek collection at the BM, I saw a lone Caryatid statue, standing in an empty alcove, roped off with tape saying it was closed to the public. This statue is one of six famous 'maidens', *korai,* designed to seemingly hold up (with their heads) the porch of the Erechtheion Temple on the Acropolis, and also taken by Elgin. The other five are in the new Acropolis Museum and well looked after, while this one looked a bit pathetic on the day of my visit. Why not at least send this one home?

It also makes no cultural sense for the BM to hold on to the Elgin heist, because the sculptures are part of an ancient narrative; mythological stories of Greek gods, their triumphs and struggles. The Parthenon frieze depicts horses, riders and athletes from the ancient Panathenaea Games procession which took place in the city every four years, and is a masterpiece. The BM holds 115 parts (247ft) of this frieze. Because of the hotchpotch of sculptures that the BM has on display, the narrative is splintered, the meaning gone.

So what might break the deadlock over the Marbles? In 2021, at a time when the call for Scottish Independence has reached a peak, with its aim to reunite Scotland ultimately with Europe again, it might have been a perfect time for the Scottish government to raise the issue of the reunification of the Parthenon sculptures itself and, more importantly, the return of the Elgin family's collection to Athens. It would be a gesture that would exonerate the Scots from this cultural heist. The Scots have not been blameless in the part they played in British colonialism, and in the slave trade, but as long as the Elgin family hold on to these Greek treasures, Scotland's reputation will be synonymous with imperial looting rather than fairness and cultural tolerance.

Dr Nikolaos Chatziandreou, a Greek research scientist who also has a background in cultural resource management, spent several years at St Andrews University and is a great admirer of Scotland and a leading proponent of reunification of the Parthenon sculptures. He believes that Scotland could certainly lead the push to get the sculptures returned. He also draws a poignant link between Scotland and Greece, between the historic struggle for the return of the Stone of Scone, once used for the coronation of Scottish monarchs, and the quest to repatriate the sculptures.

"The Acropolis sculptures are to the Greeks what the Stone of Scone is to the Scots. It is this strong historic, symbolic, emotional link between ourselves and pieces of heritage that help us define our life experience... Is it a coincidence the Stone of Scone is also called the Stone of Destiny? When it comes to the sculptures of the Acropolis, whose destiny should we see in them?" said Dr Chatziandreou.

An earlier proponent of reunification was actress and former Minister of Culture in the Greek government, Melina Mercouri, who said in 1982 the sculptures "must be reintegrated into the place and space where they were conceived. They constitute our historical and religious heritage". Although she said the British had taken the works of her ancestors, she added, "Look after them well, because the day will come when the Greeks will ask for them back."

The Greeks keep asking but no-one seems to be listening, neither the current UK government which has reiterated that the Marbles will stay in the BM, nor the current Lord Elgin in Fife. British Prime Minister Boris Johnson said in March 2021, "I understand the strong feelings of the Greek people, but the UK government has a firm, longstanding position on the sculptures, which is that they were legally acquired by Lord Elgin under the appropriate laws of the time and have been legally owned by the British Museum's Trustees since their acquisition."

And I don't hold out much hope for that lone Caryatid sister in the BM, who has become a poignant symbol of cultural intransigence. She's not holding up anything with her head now as illustrious as the Erechtheion temple, but at least she's still holding up – for now!

19

The grapes of mirth

IN rural Greece, when you leave your house for a walk around the village, the unexpected usually happens – especially if you take a dog like Wallace with you. People you haven't met before will want to stop you, to ask if it's a dog or a small sheep. To the Greek rural mind, that's what Wallace resembled, with his white body and black face. One of the unwelcome consequences of taking Wallace for a walk in Greece was that he was often a magnet for feral dogs. A small, cute, bouncy terrier on a lead – what could be better for a wild dog to annoy than that? Along with his minders.

One day in late summer we were walking along the road out of Megali Mantineia to Foteini's farm compound, as we often did, except that on this occasion, she wasn't there. Her stout front gate was padlocked. Rather than turn back, we decided to walk further along the road to where the houses petered out into thick olive groves set along the flanks of the surrounding hillside. It was a fine day and we were in no hurry to go home – until we saw a large dog skittering onto the road, barking. He began to follow us at a distance. Wallace started yapping, looking back constantly to check its progress.

The dog was a scrappy-looking thing, white with big patches of black and brown, a blocky head and thick neck, all typical of strays in rural areas, a mix of everything possible, but sturdy with it. I felt sympathy for these mutts, left to roam wild about the countryside, scavenging for food or a good a wind-up, but dangerous in the wrong circumstances. I thought the dog would get bored eventually and scram, but he kept up a brisk pursuit, getting too close to our heels and too close to Wallace. They were both growling by now, the big dog becoming snappy.

Fearing the dog would launch a proper attack, Jim picked Wallace up and tucked him under his arm. The trouble was that there was no-one around and no cars passing along the road. We felt somewhat trapped and it was a long walk back to the village. Just as we were mulling over our options, I was relieved to see a car at last, coming towards us from the village. It was a clapped-out Fiat, the kind of car rural folk kept just to drive around the village. It had no tax disk or number plates, but I recognised the driver as one of the village farmers, Hector. I waved him down.

The big dog starting barking and snapping at the car tyres. I explained to Hector about the troublesome dog and asked him where he was going.

"Not far, just up the hill there, and I'll be a while. I've got beehives there," he said, looking bemused.

"Okay, maybe we could come in the car with you, do you mind? We just want to give this feral dog the slip for a bit and later we can walk back to the village."

He grimaced comically, the way Greeks often do, meaning 'whatever!' I could tell he couldn't see what the fuss was about. Maniot farmers are bred tough. When you learn about how the Maniots once lived in tall stone towers, riven by clan vendettas, shooting at interlopers or pouring boiling oil over them from on high, outwitting the Turks for centuries, you realise that one rabid dog is no more than an annoying flea in the ear.

Before Hector could object, we piled into the back seat of the car – and I wished then we hadn't. The doors didn't seem to fit properly, as if they'd been reefed out of another vehicle. There was mess of junk inside: plastic bags of things that smelt a bit ripe, old tools, a pile of empty jars in the footwell, for the honey perhaps. We squeezed in, with Wallace on Jim's lap, and Hector set off, bumping along the road. I imagined the tyres were probably bald. It took no time at all to reach the turn-off for a narrow, steep track leading into the hills behind Megali Mantineia. Hector turned up it, the car groaning with effort and I hoped the brakes weren't rubbish as well. Seconds later, he abruptly pulled over to the side of the road.

"We're here," he said, turning towards me.

"Already?" We could have run here faster.

"I told you I wasn't going far," he said, with a sardonic grin.

Jim and I looked at each other and laughed. You had to really. We all piled out of the car.

"You can wait here if you like and come back to the village with me later. I'll just be up there," he said, pointing to a narrow terrace of land where there was a row of blue painted wooden hives.

"Okay, thanks for the lift, Hector."

Now it was his turn to guffaw at what must have seemed to him a load of theatrical faffing by a couple of *xenoi* (foreign) wimps. He set off with his bag full of bee-keeping implements, whistling as he went.

"This was such a daft idea, wasn't it?" said Jim, still holding on to Wallace because we could still see the big dog. He'd covertly run up through the olive groves from the road and was under a distant tree watching us. It was either going to have us for a late lunch, or we'd end up wearing beekeepers' suits on the hillside, waiting for Hector to return home.

We knew it would take around 45 minutes to continue up this road, which cut along the edge of the hillside, to get back to Megali Mantinea. It was a picturesque walk, yet it was also hazardous: wild boar, more feral dogs, and sometimes men in army fatigues shooting at rabbits and song birds. And the big dog was sure to give chase.

Ach, some days you should just stay in bed, I thought. That's when we heard the sound of a vehicle and looked up to see a small red tractor coming over the brow of the hill, pulling an open trailer. I was grateful to see it was Leonidas at the wheel, one of our favourite village farmers and an elder of the church. He had a nice manner and startling blue eyes and I had always jokingly called him Paul Newman.

When he was level with us, he stopped and that's when we saw the peculiar image of Foteini sitting in the trailer, dressed in a diverting outfit of clashing floral layers, a paisley headscarf topped with a straw hat. She was holding a fat bunch of grapes in her hand, feeding from it like some crazy B-grade Cleopatra out to titillate the rural masses. Jim and I chortled.

"*Yiasas paidia*!" she shouted. 'Hello guys!'

Leonidas told us he'd been up to harvest grapes from the home of an expat who currently wasn't in Greece. Foteini had come to lend a hand in return for some of the harvest and he was taking the lot back to the village. Leonidas was the kind of man who would do these jobs for other people when they weren't around or help prune their olive trees.

We told him about the feral dog. He nodded. "Yes, I've seen that one. It's a nuisance. You wouldn't want to get bitten by it. It's filthy. Climb in the back with Foteini and I'll take you all back to the village."

"Will we all fit?" I asked, eying up Foteini in the trailer and the large pile of grapes beside her. With the feral dog still visible amongst the olive trees, we didn't really have a choice.

"Climb aboard, you'll be fine," said Leonidas, smiling broadly.

Foteini quickly moved some of the grapes aside for me, while Jim had to sit opposite with Wallace on his lap. Once we'd squeezed in, I found myself sitting awkwardly on a remaining layer of grapes. I could feel the juice seeping through the seat of my jeans. Foteini continued to feast from her grape bunch but was twitchy about Wallace opposite. He never took his gimlet eyes off her, or she him. If he'd been a goat it would have been a different matter. She'd probably have offered it some grapes.

We headed back to the village, passing the big dog again on the road, having a proper strop this time at the sight of us. He barked wildly and leapt several times at the side of the trailer, baring his yellow teeth. Wallace howled back in characteristic screamy tones and then Foteini began to bark a few curses of her own and lobbed a fat bunch of grapes at the feral mutt when its face got too close to the top edge of the trailer. The dog grabbed the bunch and scarpered into the olive groves. My ears were ringing as the trailer continued to bump along the road, the grape juice seeping further into my jeans.

When we reached Foteini's *ktima* she waved Leonidas on. She wanted to go to the village shop before it closed, but I caught sight of Riko the donkey standing in the farm compound, tied to an olive tree, wearing a checked cover over his back and one of his diverting little straw hats. A mango daiquiri at his feet wouldn't have been out of the question, I mused.

Foteini saw me looking. "Nice, eh Margarita, his little *kapelaki*, to keep off the *miges* (flies)," Foteini shouted. I laughed. Of course, why not! Just another typical day for Riko, the rural fashionista.

On the outskirts of the village we drew comical looks from passers-by and a few times Leonidas had to stop to explain to curious folk what we were all doing in the trailer. I felt like I was on one of those floats you see in colourful parades for festive events. What would this 'float' take part in? Expats And Other Eccentrics Day? I imagined that later we would be the subject of light-hearted dinnertime conversation in the village, with a "*xenoi*, what are they like?" kind of comment.

We passed the house of one of our friends, Eftihia (meaning happiness), whom we had got to know well over the years. She was standing by the roadside and flagged down Leonidas, not to laugh at the motley crew in the trailer – though I clearly saw her big dark eyes crinkle with amusement – but to ask a favour. She wanted him to take some things to one of the local tavernas for her, so we waited while she went inside and brought out two stout jars filled with the pickled song birds that were a specialty in this part of the Mani and which we detested. The birds, with their heads still attached, were drifting in a viscous sea of green olive oil, a less appetising culinary image you'd be hard pressed to find. When they were handed over, Wallace barked at the imposition of dead-bird cargo. I knew how he felt.

I imagined that every time Leonidas went out with his tractor and trailer this must have happened: people wanting things dropped off, somebody wanting a lift. Well, they'd want it now!

When we eventually got out of the trailer, my back was stiff and my jeans were sticky with grape juice. Wallace had sticky paws that were clotting with grit from the roadside. He looked fizzy and hot. Foteini walk over to us with a squelch of her battered shoes. Wallace leaned down and licked the top of one of them. She offered a volley of colourful language, which I thought amusing given the usual state of her footwear. But at least she was wearing shoes and not the odd creation I'd seen her sporting once that resembled a kind of Cornish pasty. I doubt that pasties would have survived the afternoon.

We said our goodbyes and thanked Leonidas for the lift. He handed us a plastic bag bulging with grapes and smiled vibrantly. I guessed he'd found the journey highly entertaining. Foteini hugged me warmly and said goodbye. I caught the aroma of goats and oregano. Our cheeks stuck together momentarily with grape juice, which seemed somehow bizarrely symbolic.

"Come for coffee soon, to the *ktima*, Margarita. Don't forget me now." Her usual refrain.

"Sure. As soon as we can," I said, as she set off to the village shop and we turned towards home.

"*Sto kalo*!" she shouted.

'Go to the good' it means. In a Greek rural village, how can you not? Or if not to the good, at least you might point yourself towards the mad, maverick, sticky and joyous end of the moral spectrum. It's where most rural Greeks seem to live. And long may it be so!

Epilogue

I'VE been travelling around Greece on long and short trips since I first went to Athens after leaving school in the 1970s. In that time I've seen most of the mainland and many of the Greek islands. By far the most challenging and rewarding trip of all has been the one that my husband Jim and I undertook from 2010 during the Greek economic crisis. Most of our friends and family, as I have written, thought we were quite mad to set out on an odyssey at this time. Yet now, 10 years after the start of that odyssey, we are in the midst of the Covid-19 pandemic, with severe restrictions on lifestyle and travel, and ironically, we would have been madder still not to have gone on our journey when we had the chance. It turned out to be one of the best decisions we've ever made and one that changed our lives completely.

Although we've only been able to return to Greece for long holidays in recent years and not an extended stay, our previous trips to Greece, including our long odyssey, still sustain us in so many ways, especially during the punishing lockdowns imposed during the pandemic. The voyages are never forgotten and are always a source of lively discussion between Jim and me and have inspired us greatly during happy and sad times, including August 2017, when dear Wallace passed away in England, aged 16. We could rightly say that he'd had an amazing life and an odyssey that few dogs ever get a crack at. He rose to it all in a huge celebration of his own vibrant life. And few of the Greeks we met will ever forget some of Wallace's more diverting antics, which I wrote about in my memoirs.

The Greek 'journey' for me still goes on because after finishing my three memoirs I went on to write two novels in the Bronte in Greece series – *A Saint For The Summer and How Greek Is Your Love?* – also set in the Mani region, and another is planned. This collection is the fourth in my Peloponnese series.

If I've learnt nothing else from lifelong wanderings in Greece, it's this: when the opportunity to step out of your comfort zone and change your life comes your way, grab it and don't worry about the awkward, nagging details and the insecurities because "you never know what the next sunrise will bring you", to quote a Greek saying. And the chance may never come again. That applies more now than ever before as our world is turned upside down with health threats, climate emergencies and political divisions. But when the path is clear – as it will be one day – take the journey, and be thankful for every single mad thing it brings you.

THE END

Acknowledgements

Sincere thanks to all those who have inspired me to write these stories set in Greece, particularly in the Mani and Messinian peninsulas. Thanks especially to Maria and Yiorgos Bossinakis for their hospitality and for their stories of life in Falanthi, and for sharing their domestic goddess, the lovely Vera (Meropi). Also, gratitude and respect to Eleni Kostea (Foteini) and the other unique villagers of Megali Mantineia for letting me rattle about in their lives and sharing their stories. This book, as with my other memoirs, would be all the poorer without them.

Thanks also to Air Commodore Scott Miller, Commandant General, RAF Regiment, for his help in my search for information about my father John McGinn's RAF Regiment war record. The Commodore's introduction to Dr Nigel Warwick, the regiment's historian and an expert in the Mediterranean campaigns of the Second World War, was a turning point in my search. Grateful thanks to Dr Warwick for sharing operational notes for the campaigns my father fought in, including North Africa, Italy, Greece and further afield.

I'd also like to mention Greek research scientist Nikolaos Chatziandreou for eloquently drawing together some cultural links between the historic Stone of Destiny in Scotland and the Parthenon Sculptures in Greece, mentioned in the chapter Losing Our Marbles? His essay on this cultural link appears on his website www.acropolisofathens.gr

Thanks also to Scottish campaigner Tom Minogue for originally supplying observations on the Greek antiquities held at Broomhall House, Scotland.

I am hugely indebted to friend and mentor, the acclaimed Scottish author Peter Kerr for his literary advice and wisdom, and for his great good humour during my publishing adventure.

Acknowledgements

With heartfelt gratitude to my husband and fellow odyssey voyager, Jim Bruce, for his excellent editing of this book and formatting (www.ebooklover.co.uk), and his astute suggestions and enthusiasm.

And for an early reading of this book and kind comments, thanks to: Joanne Meris, Sheila Endersby, Trudi Bishop and Rebecca Hislop.

Thanks also to talented artist Anthony Hannaford for another vibrant cover illustration. (www.anthonyhannaford.co.uk)

List of photographs

The prequels

If you enjoyed this book, you might also like to read the other three best-selling books in the Peloponnese series: *Things Can Only Get Feta, Homer's Where The Heart Is* and *A Scorpion In The Lemon Tree.* These insightful and humorous memoirs explore Marjory, Jim and Wallace's adventures from the beginning, as they settle into a hillside village in southern Greece in 2010. The books chart their attempts to assimilate into Greek life as the economic crisis deepens, with an unforgettable cast of local characters, particularly the irrepressible goat farmer, Foteini. The Kindle and paperback versions are available on Amazon worldwide.

Praise for Things Can Only Get Feta

"I respectfully suggest to all wannabe authors of an 'expat life' type of book that you read this book before putting pen to paper. It's an object lesson in how it should be done. Congratulations, Marjory!" – Peter Kerr, best-selling author of *Snowball Oranges*.

"Honestly, you won't be able to put this book down."– Maria Karamitsos, reviewing in *The Greek Star* newspaper, Chicago.

"Marjory is a very talented storyteller, and many descriptions of events and turns of phrase she used in this book actually made me laugh out loud while reading silently to myself, a feat that until now was only achieved by Douglas Adams and P.G. Wodehouse." – Gry, Good Reads reviewer.

"A tale full of adventure and wit, delving into the heart of the communities in this area (Mani)... This book might become a future reference source about life in 'unspoilt' Greece." – Stella Pierides, author of *The Heart And Its Reasons*.

Praise for Homer's Where The Heart Is

"Through her stories, sentiments and humour, we see and feel her love for Greece. Put this at the top of your summer reading list." – Maria A. Karamitsos, founder and editor of *Windy City Greek*, Chicago.

"Marjory takes us on an odyssey with mind, heart and great skill. I loved reading this book." – Pamela Jane Rogers, author of *Greekscapes*.

"Another wonderful book by Marjory McGinn. The ending tugged at my heart." – Linda Fagioli-Katsiotas, author of Greek memoir, *The Nifi*.

"Marjory writes at a level that sits with the best of the travelogue genre. Her depth of characterisation and turns of phrase are outstanding." – Amazon reviewer.

Praise for A Scorpion In The Lemon Tree

"This book is rare within the travel writing genre. It cleverly combines a travel narrative with enlightened observations about Greece, while retaining a light and entertaining touch." – Peter Kerr, best-selling author of Snowball Oranges.

"Her empathy with Greece and refusal to lapse into sentimentality makes this a witty and poignant book." – Richard Clark, author of the *Greek Notebook* series.

"I absolutely love all three books in this series ... written with warmth and with humour." – Dawn, *Goodreads* reviewer.

"Fun and enlightening." – Expat Bookshop website.

The Bronte In Greece novels

A Saint For The Summer

A compelling story of heroism, faith and love

This novel, set in the wild and beautiful Mani region of southern Greece, is a contemporary story, with a cast of memorable characters. It is set during the economic crisis and combines family drama and a gripping narrative thread going back to a Second World War mystery, during the little-known Battle of Kalamata, which has been described as 'Greece's Dunkirk'. It's also a love story between the protagonist, Bronte McKnight, and the charismatic doctor, Leonidas Papachristou, with a heart-warming conclusion.

Available to buy in Kindle on Amazon. The paperback is also available through Amazon, Barnes and Noble, and other selected outlets.

Why readers love A Saint For The Summer

"I absolutely love this book. The writing is spectacular. In my opinion, this is the author's finest work." – Linda Fagioli Katsiotas, author of *The Nifi*

"Marjory McGinn is a skilful writer adept at creating characters that feel like your friends. You are reminded that all relationships can heal, that we are all connected somehow." – *Windy City Greek* magazine, Chicago

"I couldn't put this book down. The author has made the challenging transition from non-fiction to fiction. It cleverly combines elements of fact with gifted storyteller – a rare combination of skills." – Peter Kerr, best-selling author of the Mallorcan series of novels

"When I read this author's books, I walk the journeys, and with this book, I am Bronte." – Reader review

"A brilliant read … there is closure, reconciliation and the hope of new life." – Reader review

How Greek Is Your Love?

Bronte's In Love … but she's a stranger in paradise

In this sequel to *A Saint For The Summer*, expat and journalist Bronte McKnight is in the early days of her love affair with doctor Leonidas Papachristou. But as Bronte tries to live and love like a Greek, the economic crisis spawns an unlikely predator in the village. As she tries to deal with this, Bronte is offered an exclusive interview with a famous novelist and part-time expat which seems serendipitous. But the encounter becomes a puzzle that takes her deep into the Mani region, for which she enlists the help of her maverick father Angus and her newest companion, Zeffy, the rescue dog. There are more challenges still when an old love from Leonidas's past also makes a troubling appearance.

This is a page-turning story of high drama as well as humorous outcomes as Bronte tries to find a foothold in her Greek paradise. But can she succeed?

Why readers love How Greek Is Your Love?

"A captivating and skilfully crafted book that confirms Marjory McGinn as an author of popular fiction to be reckoned with." – Peter Kerr, best-selling author of the Mallorcan series

"A perfect title. This is a fast-paced story with lovable, hilarious and even frightening characters. Exciting and thought provoking." – Pamela Jane Rogers, author and artist of *Greekscapes*

"This novel is a delight from start to finish. The author is an accomplished storyteller." – Richard Clark, author of *The Lost Lyra*

"The author has done the impossible. She transported me to Greece in lockdown. A page turning story that has become my favourite read of 2020." – Reader review

"Marjory McGinn sure can write a wonderful story that holds you until the end. What a gift!" – Reader review

Printed in Great Britain
by Amazon